Joel
A Boy Of Galilee

Annie F. Johnston

Alpha Editions

This Edition Published in 2020

ISBN: 9789354365393

Design and Setting By
Alpha Editions
www.alphaedis.com
Email – info@alphaedis.com

As per information held with us this book is in Public Domain.
This book is a reproduction of an important historical work. Alpha Editions uses the best technology to reproduce historical work in the same manner it was first published to preserve its original nature. Any marks or number seen are left intentionally to preserve its true form.

PUBLISHER'S PREFACE

IN this volume, it has been the purpose of the author to present to children, through " Joel," as accurate a picture of the times of the Christ as has been given to older readers through " Ben Hur." With this in view, the customs of the private and public life of the Jews, the temple service with its sacerdotal rites, and the minute observances of the numerous holidays have been studied so carefully that the descriptions have passed the test of the most critical inspection. An eminent rabbi pronounces them correct in every detail.

While the story is that of an ordinary boy, living among shepherds and fishermen, it touches at every point the gospel narrative, making Joel, in a natural and interesting way, a witness to the miracles, the death, and the resurrection of the Nazarene.

It was with the deepest reverence that the task was undertaken, and the fact that the little book is accomplishing its mission is evinced not only by the approval accorded its first editions by so many, from Bible students to bishops, but by the boys and girls here and in distant lands.

LIST OF ILLUSTRATIONS

	PAGE
"'THEN TAKE YOURSELF OUT OF MY SIGHT FOR EVER'" (*See page 96*) . . . . *Frontispiece*	
"HE LOOKED DOWN AT PHINEAS, AND SMILED BLISSFULLY"	34
"'I PEEPED OUT 'TWEEN 'E WOSE-VINES'" . .	82
"NOT A WORD WAS SAID"	104
"'WE TALKED LATE'"	139
"'YOU BUT MOCK ME, BOY'"	184
"A DARK FIGURE WENT SKULKING OUT INTO THE NIGHT"	203
"'THE STONE IS GONE!'"	233

JOEL: A BOY OF GALILEE.

CHAPTER I.

T was market day in Capernaum. Country people were coming in from the little villages among the hills of Galilee, with fresh butter and eggs. Fishermen held out great strings of shining perch and carp, just dipped up from the lake beside the town. Vine-dressers piled their baskets with tempting grapes, and boys lazily brushed the flies from the dishes of wild honey, that they had gone into the country before day-break to find.

A ten-year-old girl pushed her way through the crowded market-place, carrying her baby brother in her arms, and scolding another child, who clung to her skirts.

"Hurry, you little snail!" she said to him. "There's a camel caravan just stopped by the custom-house. Make haste, if you want to see it!"

Their bare feet picked their way quickly over the stones, down to the hot sand of the lake shore. The children crept close to the shaggy camels, curious to see what they carried in their huge packs. But before they were made to kneel, so that the custom-house officials could examine the loads, the boy gave an exclamation of surprise.

"Look, Jerusha! Look!" he cried, tugging at her skirts. "What's that?"

Farther down the line, came several men carrying litters. On each one was a man badly wounded, judging by the many bandages that wrapped him.

Jerusha pushed ahead to hear what had happened. One of the drivers was telling a tax-gatherer.

"In that last rocky gorge after leaving Samaria," said the man, "we were set upon by robbers. They swarmed down the cliffs, and fought as fiercely as eagles. These men, who were going on ahead, had much gold with them. They lost it all, and might have been killed, if we had not come up behind in such numbers. That poor fellow there can hardly live, I think, he was beaten so badly."

The children edged up closer to the motionless form on the litter. It was badly bruised and blood-stained, and looked already lifeless.

"Let's go, Jerusha," whispered the boy, whimpering and pulling at her hand. "I don't like to look at him."

With the heavy baby still in her arms, and the other child tagging after, she started slowly back towards the market-place.

"I'll tell you what we'll do," she exclaimed. "Let's go up and get the other children, and play robbers. We never did do that before. It will be lots of fun."

There was a cry of welcome as Jerusha appeared again in the market-place, where a crowd of children were playing tag, regardless of the men and beasts they bumped against. They were all younger than herself, and did not resent her important air when she called, "Come here! I know a better game than that!"

She told them what she had just seen and heard down at the beach, and drew such a vivid picture of the attack, that the children were ready for anything she might propose.

"Now we'll choose sides," she said. "I'll be a rich merchant coming up from Jerusalem with my family and servants, and the rest of you can be robbers. We'll go along with our goods, and you pounce out on us as we go by. You may take the baby as a prisoner if you like," she added, with a mischievous grin. "I'm tired of carrying him."

A boy sitting near by on a door-step, jumped up eagerly. "Let me play, too, Jerusha!" he cried. "I'll be one of the robbers. I know just the best places to hide!"

The girl paused an instant in her choosing to say impatiently, although not meaning to be unkind, "Oh, no, Joel! We do not want you. You're too lame to run. You can't play with us!"

The bright, eager look died out of the boy's face, and an angry light shone in his eyes. He pressed his lips together hard, and sat down again on the step.

There was a patter of many bare feet as the children raced away. Their voices sounded fainter and fainter, till they were lost entirely in the noise of the busy street.

Usually, Joel found plenty to amuse and interest him here. He liked to watch the sleepy donkeys with their loads of fresh fruit and vegetables. He liked to listen to the men as they cried their wares, or chatted over the bargains with their customers. There was always something new to be seen in the stalls and booths. There was always something new to be heard in the scraps of conversation that came to him where he sat.

Down this street there sometimes came long caravans; for this was "the highway to the sea,"— the road that led from Egypt to Syria. Strange, dusky faces sometimes passed this way; richly dressed merchant princes with their priceless stuffs from beyond the Nile; heavy loads of Babylonian carpets; pearls from Ceylon, and rich silks for the court of the wicked Herodias, in the town beyond. Fisherman and sailor, rabbi and busy workman passed in an endless procession.

Sometimes a Roman soldier from the garrison came by with ringing step and clanking sword. Then Joel would start up to look after the erect figure, with a longing gaze that told more plainly than words, his admiration of such strength and symmetry.

But this morning the crowd gave him a strange, lonely feeling, — a hungry longing for companionship.

Two half-grown boys passed by on their way to the lake, with fish nets slung over their shoulders. He knew the larger one, — a rough, kind-hearted fellow who had once taken him in his boat across the lake. He gave Joel a careless, good-natured nod as he passed. A moment after he felt a timid pull at the fish net he was carrying, and turned to see the little cripple's appealing face.

"Oh, Dan!" he cried eagerly. "Are you going out on the lake this morning? Could you take me with you?"

The boy hesitated. Whatever kindly answer he may have given, was rudely interrupted by his companion, whom Joel had never seen before.

"Oh, no!" he said roughly. "We don't want anybody limping along after us. You can't come, Jonah; you would bring us bad luck."

"My name is n't Jonah!" screamed the boy, angrily clinching his fists. "It's Joel!"

"Well, it is all the same," his tormentor called back, with a coarse laugh. "You're a Jonah, any way."

There were tears in the boy's eyes this time, as he dragged himself back again to the step.

"I hate everybody in the world!" he said in a hissing sort of whisper. "I hate 'm! I hate 'm!"

A stranger passing by turned for a second look at the little cripple's sensitive, refined face. A girlishly beautiful face it would have been, were it not for the heavy scowl that darkened it.

Joel pulled the ends of his head-dress round to hide his crooked back, and drew the loose robe he wore over his twisted leg.

Life seemed very bitter to him just then. He would gladly have changed places with the heavily laden donkey going by.

"I wish I were dead," he thought moodily. "Then I would not ache any more, and I could not hear when people call me names!"

Beside the door where he sat was a stand where tools and hardware were offered for sale. A man who had been standing there for some time, selecting nails from the boxes placed before him, and had heard all that passed, spoke to him.

"Joel, my lad, may I ask your help for a little while?" The friendly question seemed to change the whole atmosphere.

Joel drew his hands across his eyes to clear them of the blur of tears he was too proud to let fall, and then stood up respectfully. "Yes, Rabbi Phineas, what would you have me to do?"

The carpenter gathered up some strips of lumber in one hand, and his hammer and saws in the other.

"I have my hands too full to carry these nails," he answered. "If you could bring them for me, it would be a great service."

If the man had offered him pity, Joel would have fiercely resented it. His sensitive nature appreciated the unspoken sympathy, the fine tact that soothed his pride by asking a service of him, instead of seeking to render one.

He could not define the feeling, but he gratefully took up the bag of nails, and limped along beside his friend to the carpenter's house at the edge of the town. He had never been there before, although he met the man daily in the market-place, and long ago had learned to look forward to his pleasant greeting; it was so different from most people's. Somehow the morning always seemed brighter after he had met him.

The little whitewashed house stood in the shade of two great fig-trees near the beach. A cool breeze from the Galilee lifted the leaves, and swayed the vines growing around the low door.

Joel, tired by the long walk, was glad to throw himself on the grass in the shade. It was so still and quiet here, after the noise of the street he had just left.

An old hen clucked around the door-step with a brood of downy, yellow chickens. Doves cooed softly, somewhere out of sight. The carpenter's bench stood under one of the trees, with shavings and chips all around it. Two children were playing near it, building houses of the scattered blocks; one of them, a black-eyed, sturdy boy of five, kept on playing. The other, a little girl, not yet three, jumped up and followed her father into the house. Her curls gleamed like gold as she ran through the sunshine. She glanced at the stranger with deep-blue eyes so like her father's that Joel held out his hand.

"Come and tell me your name," he said coaxingly. But she only shook the curls all over her dimpled face, and hurried into the house.

"It's Ruth," said the boy, deigning to look up. "And mine is Jesse, and my mother's is Abigail, and my father's is Phineas, and my grand-father's is — "

How far back he would have gone in his genealogy, Joel could not guess; for just then his father came out with a cool, juicy melon, and Jesse hurried forward to get his share.

"How good it is!" sighed Joel, as the first refreshing mouthful slipped down his thirsty throat. "And how cool and pleasant it is out here. I did not know there was such a peaceful spot in all Capernaum."

"Did n't you always live here?" asked the inquisitive Jesse.

"No, I was born in Jerusalem. I was to have been a priest," he said sadly.

"Well, why did n't you be one then," persisted the child, with his mouth full of melon.

Joel glanced down at his twisted leg, and said nothing.

"Why?" repeated the boy.

Phineas, who had gone back to his work-bench, looked up kindly. "You ask too many questions, my son. No one can be a priest who is maimed or blemished in any way. Some sad accident must have befallen our little friend, and it may be painful for him to talk about it."

Jesse asked no more questions with his tongue; but his sharp, black eyes were fixed on Joel like two interrogation points.

"I do not mind telling about it," said Joel, sitting up straighter. "Once when I was not much older than you, just after my mother died, my father brought me up to this country from Jerusalem, to visit my Aunt Leah.

"I used to play down here by the lake, with my cousins, in the fishermen's boats. There was a boy that came to the beach sometimes, a great deal larger than I, — a dog of a Samaritan, — who pulled my hair and threw sand in my eyes. He was so much stronger than I, that I could not do anything to him but call him names. But early one morning he was swimming in the lake. I hid his clothes in the oleander bushes that fringe the water. Oh, but he was angry! I wanted him to be. But I had to keep away from the lake after that.

"One day some older children took me to the hills back of the town to gather almonds. This Rehum followed us. I had strayed away from the others a little distance, and was stooping to put the nuts in my basket, when he slipped up behind me. How he beat me! I screamed so that the other children came running back to me. When he saw them coming, he gave me a great push that sent me rolling over a rocky bank. It was not very high, but there were sharp stones below.

"They thought I was dead when they picked me up. It was months before I could walk at all; and I can never be an any better than I am now. Just as my father was about to take me back to Jerusalem, he took a sudden fever, and died. So I was left, a poor helpless burden for my aunt to take care of. It has been six years since then."

Joel threw himself full length on the grass, and scowled up at the sky.

"Where is that boy that hurt you," asked Jesse.

"Rehum?" questioned Joel. "I wish I knew," he muttered fiercely. "Oh, how I hate him! I can never be a priest as my father intended. I can never serve in the beautiful temple with the white pillars and golden gates. I can never be like other people, but must drag along, deformed and full of pain as long as I live. And it's all his fault!"

A sudden gleam lit up the boy's eyes, as lightning darts through a storm-cloud.

"But I shall have my revenge!" he added, clinching his fists. "I cannot die till I have made him feel at least a tithe of what I have suffered. 'An eye for an eye, and a tooth for a tooth!' That is the least that can satisfy me. Oh, you cannot know how I long for that time! Often I lie awake late into the night, planning my revenge. Then I forget how my back hurts and my leg pains; then I forget all the names I have been called, and the taunts that make my life a burden. But they all come back with the daylight; and I store them up and add them to his account. For everything he has made me suffer, I swear he shall pay for it four-fold in his own sufferings!"

Ruth shrank away, frightened by the wild, impassioned boy who sat up, angrily staring in front of him with eyes that saw nothing of the sweet, green-clad world around him. The face of his enemy blotted out all the sunny landscape. One murderous purpose filled him, mind and soul.

Nothing was said for a little while. The doves as before cooed of peace, and Phineas began a steady tap-tap with his hammer.

A pleasant-faced woman came out of the door with a water-jar on her head, and passed down the path to the public well. She gave Joel a friendly greeting in passing.

"Wait, mother!" lisped Ruth, as she ran after her. The woman turned to smile at the little one, and held out her hand. Her dress, of some soft, cotton material, hung in long flowing folds. It was a rich blue color, caught at the waist with a white girdle. The turban wound around her dark hair was white also, and so was the veil she pushed aside far enough to show a glimpse of brown eyes and red cheeks. She wore a broad silver bracelet on the bare arm which was raised to hold the water-jar, and the rings in her ears and talismans on her neck were of quaintly wrought silver.

"I did not know it was so late," said Joel, rising to his feet. "Time passes so fast here."

"Nay, do not go," said Phineas. "It is a long walk back to your home, and the sun is very hot. Stay and eat dinner with us."

Joel hesitated; but the invitation was repeated so cordially, that he let Jesse pull him down on the grass again.

"Now I'll tickle your lips with this blade of grass," said the child. "See how long you can keep from laughing."

When Abigail came back with the water, both the boys were laughing as heartily as if there had never been an ache or pain in the world. She smiled at them approvingly, as she led the way into the house.

Joel looked around with much curiosity. It was like most of the other houses of its kind in the town. There was only one large square room, in which the family cooked, ate, and slept; but on every side it showed that Phineas had left traces of his skilful hands.

There was a tiny window cut in one wall; most of the houses of this description had none, but depended on the doorway for light and air. Several shelves around the walls held the lamp and the earthenware dishes. The chest made to hold the rugs and cushions which they spread down at night to sleep on, was unusually large and ornamental. A broom, a handmill, and a bushel stood in one corner.

Near the door, a table which Phineas had made, stood spread for the mid-day meal.

There was broiled fish on one of the platters, beans and barley bread, a dish of honey, and a pitcher of milk. The fare was just the same that Joel was accustomed to in his uncle's house; but something made the simple meal seem like a banquet. It may have been that the long walk had made him hungrier than usual, or it may have been because he was treated as the honored guest, instead of a child tolerated through charity.

He watched his host carefully, as he poured the water over his hands before eating, and asked a blessing on the food.

"He does not keep the law as strictly as my Uncle Laban," was his inward comment. "He asked only one blessing, and Uncle Laban blesses every kind of food separately. But he must be a good man, even if he is not so strict a Pharisee as my uncle, for he is kinder than any one I ever knew before."

It was wonderful how much Joel had learned, in his eleven short years, of the Law. His aunt's husband had grown to manhood in Jerusalem, and, unlike the simple Galileans among whom he now lived, tried to observe its most detailed rules.

The child heard them discussed continually, till he felt he could neither eat, drink, nor dress, except by these set rules. He could not play like other children, and being so much with older people had made him thoughtful and observant.

He had learned to read very early; and hour after hour he spent in the house of Rabbi Amos, the most learned man of the town, poring over his rolls of scriptures. Think of a childhood without a picture, or a story-book! All that there was to read were these old records of Jewish history.

The old man had taken a fancy to him, finding him an appreciative listener and an apt pupil. So Joel was allowed to come whenever he pleased, and take out the yellow rolls of parchment from their velvet covers.

He was never perfectly happy except at these times, when he was reading these old histories of his country's greatness. How he enjoyed chasing the armies of the Philistines, and fighting over again the battles of Israel's kings! Many a tale he stored away in his busy brain to be repeated to the children gathered around the public fountain in the cool of the evening.

It mattered not what character he told them of, — priest or prophet, judge or king, — the picture was painted in life-like colors by this patriotic little hero-worshipper.

Here and at home he heard so many discussions about what was lawful and what was not, that he was constantly in fear of breaking one of the many rules, even in as simple a duty as washing a cup.

So he watched his host closely till the meal was over, finding that in the observance of many customs, he failed to measure up to his uncle's strict standard.

Phineas went back to his work after dinner. He was greatly interested in Joel, and, while he sawed and hammered, kept a watchful eye on him. He was surprised at the boy's knowledge. More than once he caught himself standing with an idle tool in hand, as he listened to some story that Joel was telling to Jesse.

After a while he laid down his work and leaned against the bench. "What do you find to do all day, my lad?" he asked, abruptly.

"Nothing," answered Joel, "after I have recited my lessons to Rabbi Amos."

"Does your aunt never give you any tasks to do at home?"

"No. I think she does not like to have me in her sight any more than she is obliged to. She is always kind to me, but she does n't love me. She only pities me. I hate to be pitied. There is not a single one in the world who really loves me."

His lips quivered, but he winked back the tears. Phineas seemed lost in thought a few minutes; then he looked up. "You are a Levite," he said slowly, "so of course you could always be supported without needing to learn a trade. Still you would be a great deal happier, in my opinion, if you had something to keep you busy. If you like, I will teach you to be a carpenter. There are a great many things you might learn to make well, and, by and by, it would be a source of profit to you. There is no bread so bitter as the bread of dependence, as you may learn when you are older."

"Oh, Rabbi Phineas!" cried Joël. "Do you mean that I may come here every day? It is too good to be true!"

"Yes; if you will promise to stick to it until you have mastered the trade. If you are as quick to learn with your hands as you have been with your head, I shall have reason to be proud of such a pupil."

Joel's face flushed with pleasure, and he sprang up quickly, saying, "May I begin right now? Oh, I'll try *so* hard to please you!"

Phineas laid a soft pine board on the bench, and began to mark a line across it with a piece of red chalk.

"Well, you may see how straight a cut you can make through this plank."

He picked up a saw, and ran his fingers lightly along its sharp teeth. But he paused in the act of handing it to Joel, to ask, "You are sure, now, that your uncle and aunt will consent to such an arrangement?"

"Yes indeed!" was the emphatic answer. "They will be glad enough to have me out of the way, and learning something useful."

The saw cut slowly through the wood; for the weak little hand was a careful one, and the boy was determined not to swerve once from the line. He smiled with satisfaction as the pieces fell apart, showing a clean, straight edge.

"Well done!" said Phineas, kindly. "Now let me see you drive a nail." Made bold by his first success, Joel pounded away vigorously, but the hammer slipped more than once, and his unpractised fingers ached with the blows that he had aimed at the nail's head.

"You'll soon learn," said Phineas, with an encouraging pat on the boy's shoulder. "Gather up those odds and ends under the bench. When you've sawed them into equal lengths, I'll show you how to make a box."

Joel bent over his work with almost painful intensity. He fairly held his breath, as he made the measurements. He gripped the saw as if his life depended on the strength of his hold. Phineas smiled at his earnestness.

"Be careful, my lad," he said. "You will soon wear out at that rate."

It seemed to Joel that there never had been such a short afternoon. He had stopped to rest several times, when Phineas had insisted upon it; but this new work had all the fascination of an interesting game. The trees threw giant shadows across the grass, when he finally laid his tools aside. His back ached with so much unusual exercise, and he was very tired.

"Rabbi Phineas," he asked gently, after a long pause, "what makes you so good to me? What makes you so different from other people? While I am with you, I feel like I want to be good. Other people seem to rub me the wrong way, and make me cross and hateful; then I feel like I'd rather be wicked than not. Why this afternoon, I've scarcely thought of Rehum at all. I forgot at times that I am lame. When you talk to me, I feel like I did that day Dan took me out on the lake. It seemed a different kind of a world, — all blue sky and smooth water. I felt if I could stay out there all the time, where it was so quiet and comforting, that I could not even hate Rehum as much as I do."

A surprised, pleased look passed over the man's face. "Do I really make you feel that way, little one? Then I am indeed glad. Once when I was a young boy living in Nazareth, I had a playmate who had that influence over me and all the boys he played with. I never could be selfish and impatient when he was with me. His very presence rebuked such thoughts, — when we were children playing together, like my own two little ones there, and when we were older grown, working at the same bench. It has been many a long year since I left Nazareth, but I think of him daily. Even now, after our long separation, the thought of his blameless life inspires me to a higher living. Yes," he went on musingly, more to himself than the boy, "it was like music. Surely no white-robed priest in the holy temple ever offered up more acceptable praise than the perfect harmony of his daily life."

Joel's lips trembled. "If I had ever had one real friend to care for me — not just pity me, you know — maybe I would have been different. But I have never had a single one since my father died."

Phineas smiled, and held out his hand. "You have one now, my lad, never forget that."

The strong brown hand closed in a warm grasp, and Joel drew it, with a grateful impulse, to his lips. Ruth came up with wondering eyes. She could not understand what had passed; but Joel's eyes were full of tears, and she vaguely felt that he needed comfort. She had a pet pigeon in her arms, that she carried everywhere with her.

"Here," she lisped, holding out the snowy winged bird. "Boy, take it! Boy, keep it!"

Joel looked up inquiringly at Phineas. "Take it," he said, in a low tone. "Let it be the omen of a happier life commencing for you."

"I never had a pet of any kind before," said Joel, in delight, smoothing the white wings folded contentedly against his breast. "But she loves it so, I dislike to take it from her. How beautiful it is!"

"My little Ruth is a born comforter," said Phineas, tossing her up in his arms. "Shall Joel take the pigeon home with him, little daughter?"

"Yes," she answered, nodding her head. "Boy cried."

"I'll name it 'Little Friend,'" said Joel, rising with it in his arms. "I'll take it home with me, and keep it until after the Sabbath, to make me feel sure that this day has not been just a dream; but I will bring it back next time I come. I can see it here every day, and it will be happier here. Oh, Rabbi Phineas, I can never thank you enough for this day!"

It was a pitiful little figure that limped away homeward in the fading light, with the white pigeon in his arms.

Looking anxiously up in the sky, Joel saw one star come twinkling out. The Sabbath would soon begin, and then he must not be found carrying even so much as this one poor little pigeon. The slightest burden would be unlawful.

As he hurried on, the loud blast of a trumpet, blown from the roof of the synagogue, signalled the laborers in the fields to stop all work. He knew that very soon it would sound again, to call the town people from their tasks; and at the third blast, the Sabbath lamp would be lighted in every home.

Fearful of his uncle's displeasure at his tardiness, he hurried painfully onward, to provide food and a resting-place for his " little friend" before the second sounding of the trumpet.

CHAPTER II.

ARLY in the morning after the Sabbath, Joel was in his accustomed place in the market, waiting for his friend Phineas. His uncle had given a gruff assent, when he timidly asked his approval of the plan.

The good Rabbi Amos was much pleased when he heard of the arrangement. "Thou hast been a faithful student," he said, kindly. "Thou knowest already more of the Law than many of thy elders. Now it will do thee good to learn the handicraft of Phineas. Remember, my son, 'the balm was created by God before the wound.' Work, that is as old as Eden, has been given us that we might forget the afflictions of this life that fleeth like a shadow. May the God of thy fathers give thee peace!"

With the old man's benediction repeating itself like a solemn refrain in all his thoughts, Joel stood smoothing the pigeon in his arms, until Phineas had made his daily purchases

Then they walked on together in the cool of the morning, to the little white house under the fig-trees. Phineas was surprised at his pupil's progress. To be sure, the weak arms could lift little, the slender hands could attempt no large tasks. But the painstaking care he bestowed on everything he attempted, resulted in beautifully finished work. If there was an extra smooth polish to be put on some wood, or a delicate piece of joining to do, Joel's deft fingers seemed exactly suited to the task.

Before the winter was over, he had made many pretty little articles of furniture for Abigail's use.

"May I have these pieces of fine wood to use as I please?" he asked of Phineas, one day.

"All but that largest strip," he answered. "What are you going to make?"

"Something for Ruth's birthday. She will be three years old in a few weeks, Jesse says, and I want to make something for her to play with."

"What are you going to make her?" inquired Jesse, from under the work-bench. "Let me see too."

"Oh, I didn't know you were anywhere near," answered Joel, with a start of alarm.

"Tell me!" begged Jesse.

"Well, if you will promise to keep her out of the way while I am finishing it, and never say a word about it—"

"I'll promise," said the child, solemnly. He had to clap his hand over his mouth a great many times in the next few weeks, to keep his secret from telling itself, and he watched admiringly while Joel carved and polished and cut.

One of the neighbors had come in to talk with Abigail the day he finished it, and as the children were down on the beach, playing in the sand, he took it in the house to show to the women. It was a little table set with toy dishes, that he had carved out of wood, — plates and cups and platters, all complete.

The visitor held up her hands with an exclamation of delight. After taking up each little highly polished dish to admire it separately, she said, "I know where you might get a great deal of money for such work. There is a rich Roman living near the garrison, who spends money like a lord. No price is too great for him to pay for anything that pleases his fancy. Why don't you take some up there, and offer them for sale?"

"I believe I will," said Joel, after considering the matter. "I'll go just as soon as I can get them made."

Ruth spread many a little feast under the fig-trees; but after the first birthday banquet, Jesse was her only guest. Joel was too busy making more dishes and another little table, to partake of them.

The whole family were interested in his success. The day he went up to the great house near the garrison to offer them for sale, they waited anxiously for his return.

"He's sold them! He's sold them!" cried Jesse, hopping from one foot to the other, as he saw Joel coming down the street empty-handed. Joel was hobbling along as fast as he could, his face beaming.

"See how much money!" he cried, as he opened his hand to show a shining coin, stamped with the head of Cæsar. "And I have an order for two more. I'll soon have a fortune! The children liked the dishes so much, although they had the most beautiful toys I ever saw. They had images they called dolls. Some of them had white-kid faces, and were dressed as richly as queens. I wish Ruth had one."

"The law forbids!" exclaimed Phineas. "Have you forgotten that it is written, 'Thou shalt not make any likeness of anything in the heavens above or the earth beneath, or the waters under the earth'? She is happy with what she has, and needs no strange idols of the heathen to play with."

Joel made no answer; but he thought of the merry group of Roman children seated around the little table he had made, and wished again that Ruth had one of those gorgeously dressed dolls.

Skill and strength were not all he gained by his winter's work; for some of the broad charity that made continual summer in the heart of Phineas crept into his own embittered nature. He grew less suspicious of those around him, and smiles came more easily now to his face than scowls.

But the strong ambition of his life never left him for an instant. To all the rest of the world he might be a friend; to Rehum he could only be the most unforgiving of enemies.

The thought that had given him most pleasure when the wealthy Roman had tossed him his first earnings, was not that his work could bring him money, but that the money could open the way for his revenge.

That thought, like a dark undercurrent, gained depth and force as the days went by. As he saw how much he could do in spite of his lameness, he thought of how much more he might have accomplished, if he had been like other boys. It was a constant spur to his desire for revenge.

One day Phineas laid aside his tools much earlier than usual, and without any explanation to his wondering pupil, went up into the town.

When he returned, he nodded to his wife, who sat in the doorway spinning, and who had looked up inquiringly as he approached.

"Yes, it's all arranged," he said to her. Then he turned to Joel to ask, "Did you ever ride on a camel, my boy?"

"No, Rabbi," answered the boy, in surprise, wondering what was coming next.

"Well, I have a day's journey to make to the hills in Upper Galilee. A camel caravan passes near the place where my business calls me, as it goes to Damascus. I seek to accompany it for protection. I go on foot, but I have made arrangements for you to ride one of the camels."

"Oh, am I really to go, too?" gasped Joel, in delighted astonishment. "Oh, Rabbi Phineas! How did you ever think of asking me?"

"You have not seemed entirely well, of late," was the answer. "I thought the change would do you good. I said nothing about it before, for I had no opportunity to see your uncle until this afternoon; and I did not want to disappoint you, in case he refused his permission."

"And he really says I may go?" demanded the boy, eagerly.

"Yes, the caravan moves in the morning, and we will go with it."

There was little more work done that day. Joel was so full of anticipations of his journey that he scarcely knew what he was doing. Phineas was busy with preparations for the comfort of his little family during his absence, and went into town again.

On his return he seemed strangely excited. Abigail, seeing something was amiss, watched him carefully, but asked no questions. He took a piece of timber that had been laid away for some especial purpose, and began sawing it into small bits.

"Rabbi Phineas," ventured Joel, respectfully, "is that not the wood you charged me to save so carefully?"

Phineas gave a start as he saw what he had done, and threw down his saw.

"Truly," he said, smiling, "I am beside myself with the news I have heard. I just now walked ten cubits past my own house, unknowing where I was, so deeply was I thinking upon it. Abigail," he asked, "do you remember my friend in Nazareth whom I so often speak of, — the son of Joseph the carpenter? Last week he was bidden to a marriage in Cana. It happened, before the feasting was over, the supply of wine was exhausted, and the mortified host knew not what to do. Six great jars of stone had been placed in the room, to supply the guests with water for washing. *He changed that water into wine!*"

"I cannot believe it!" answered Abigail, simply.

"But Ezra ben Jared told me so. He was there, and drank of the wine," insisted Phineas.

"He could not have done it," said Abigail, "unless he were helped by the evil one, or unless he were a prophet. He is too a good man to ask help of the powers of darkness; and it is beyond belief that a son of Joseph should be a prophet."

To this Phineas made no answer. His quiet thoughts were shaken out of their usual routine as violently as if by an earthquake.

Joel thought more of the journey than he did of the miracle. It seemed to the impatient boy that the next day never would dawn. Many times in the night he wakened to hear the distant crowing of cocks. At last, by straining his eyes he could distinguish the green leaves of the vine on the lattice from the blue of the half-opened blossoms. By that token he knew it was near enough the morning for him to commence saying his first prayers.

Dressing noiselessly, so as not to disturb the sleeping family, he slipped out of the house and down to the well outside the city-gate. Here he washed, and then ate the little lunch he had wrapped up the night before. A meagre little breakfast, — only a hard-boiled egg, a bit of fish, and some black bread. But the early hour and his excitement took away his appetite for even that little.

Soon all was confusion around the well, as the noisy drivers gathered to water their camels, and make their preparations for the start.

Joel shrunk away timidly to the edge of the crowd, fearful that his friend Phineas had overslept himself.

In a few minutes he saw him coming with a staff in one hand, and a small bundle swinging from the other.

Joel had one breathless moment of suspense as he was helped on to the back of the kneeling camel; one desperate clutch at the saddle as the huge animal plunged about and rose to its feet.

Then he looked down at Phineas, and smiled blissfully.

Oh, the delight of that slow easy motion! The joy of being carried along without pain or effort! Who could realize how much it meant to the little fellow whose halting steps had so long been taken in weariness and suffering?

Swinging along in the cool air, so far above the foot-passengers, it seemed to him that he looked down upon a new earth. Blackbirds flew along the roads, startled by their passing. High overhead, a lark had not yet finished her morning song. Lambs bleated in the pastures, and the lowing of herds sounded on every hill-side.

Not a sight or sound escaped the boy; and all the morning he rode on without speaking, not a care in his heart, not a cloud on his horizon.

At noon they stopped in a little grove of olive-trees where a cool spring gurgled out from the rocks.

Phineas spread out their lunch at a little distance from the others; and they ate it quickly, with appetites sharpened by the morning's travel. Afterwards Joel stretched himself out on the ground to rest, and was asleep almost as soon as his eyelids could shut out the noontide glare of the sun from his tired eyes.

"HE LOOKED DOWN AT PHINEAS, AND SMILED BLISSFULLY"

When he awoke, nearly an hour afterward, he heard voices near him in earnest conversation. Raising himself on his elbow, he saw Phineas at a little distance, talking to an old man who had ridden one of the foremost camels.

They must have been talking of the miracle, for the old man, as he stroked his long white beard, was saying, "But men are more wont to be astonished at the sun's eclipse, than at his daily rising. Look, my friend!"

He pointed to a wild grape-vine clinging to a tree near by. "Do you see those bunches of half-grown grapes? There is a constant miracle. Day by day, the water of the dew and rain is being changed into the wine of the grape. Soil and sunshine are turning into fragrant juices. Yet you feel no astonishment."

"No," assented Phineas; "for it is by the hand of God it is done."

"Why may not this be also?" said the old man. "Even this miracle at the marriage feast in Cana?"

Phineas started violently. "What!" he cried. "Do you think it possible that this friend of mine is the One to be sent of God?"

"Is not this the accepted time for the coming of Israel's Messiah?" answered the old man, solemnly. " Is it not meet that he should herald his presence by miracles and signs and wonders?"

Joel lay down again to think over what he had just heard. Like every other Israelite in the whole world, he knew that a deliverer had been promised his people.

Time and again he had read the prophecies that foretold the coming of a king through the royal line of David; time and again he had pictured to himself the mighty battles to take place between his down-trodden race and the haughty hordes of Cæsar. Sometime, somewhere, a universal dominion awaited them. He firmly believed that the day was near at hand; but not even in his wildest dreams had he ever dared to hope that it might come in his own lifetime.

He raised himself on his elbow again, for the old man was speaking.

"About thirty years ago," he said slowly, " I went up to Jerusalem to be registered for taxation, for the emperor's decree had gone forth and no one could escape enrolment. You are too young to remember the taking of that census, my friend; but you have doubtless heard of it."

" Yes," assented Phineas, respectfully.

"I was standing just outside the Joppa gate, bargaining with a man for a cage of gold finches he had for sale, which I wished to take to my daughter, when we heard some one speaking to us. Looking up we saw several strange men on camels, who were inquiring their way. They were richly dressed. The trappings and silver bells on their camels, as well as their own attire, spoke of wealth. Their faces showed that they were wise and learned men from far countries.

"We greeted them respectfully, but could not speak for astonishment when we heard their question:

"'Where is he that is born king of the Jews? For we have seen his star in the East, and have come to worship him.' The bird-seller looked at me, and I looked at him in open-mouthed wonder. The men rode on before we could find words wherewith to answer them.

"All sorts of rumors were afloat, and everywhere we went next day, throughout Jerusalem, knots of people stood talking of the mysterious men, and their strange question. Even the king was interested, and sought audience with them."

"Could any one answer them?" asked Phineas.

"Nay! but it was then impressed on me

so surely that the Christ was born, that I have asked myself all these thirty years, 'Where is he that is born king of the Jews?' For I too would fain follow on to find and worship him. As soon as I return from Damascus, I shall go at once to Cana, and search for this miracle-worker."

The old man's earnest words made a wonderful impression on Joel. All the afternoon, as they rose higher among the hills, the thought took stronger possession of him. He might yet live, helpless little cripple as he was, to see the dawn of Israel's deliverance, and a son of David once more on its throne.

Ride on, little pilgrim, happy in thy day-dreams! The time is coming; but weary ways and hopeless heart-aches lie between thee and that to-morrow. The king is on his way to his coronation, but it will be with thorns.

Ride on, little pilgrim, be happy whilst thou can!

CHAPTER III.

T was nearly the close of the day when the long caravan halted, and tents were pitched for the night near a little brook that came splashing down from a cold mountain-spring.

Joel, exhausted by the long day's travel, crowded so full of new experiences, was glad to stretch his cramped limbs on a blanket that Phineas took from the camel's back.

Here, through half-shut eyes, he watched the building of the camp-fire, and the preparations for the evening meal.

"I wonder what Uncle Laban would do if he were here!" he said to Phineas, with an amused smile. "Look at those dirty drivers with their unwashed hands and unblessed food. How little regard they have for the Law. Uncle Laban would fast a lifetime rather than taste anything that had even been passed over a fire of their building. I can imagine I see him now, gathering up his skirts and walking on the tips of his sandals for fear of being touched by anything unclean."

"Your Uncle Laban is a good man," answered Phineas, "one careful not to transgress the Law."

"Yes," said the boy. "But I like your way better. You keep the fasts, and repeat the prayers, and love God and your neighbors. Uncle Laban is careful to do the first two things; I am not so sure about the others. Life is too short to be always washing one's hands."

Phineas looked at the little fellow sharply. How shrewd and old he seemed for one of his years! Such independence of thought was unusual in a child trained as he had been. He scarcely knew how to answer him, so he turned his attention to spreading out the fruits and bread he had brought for their supper.

Next morning, after the caravan had gone on without them, they started up a narrow bridle-path, that led through hillside-pastures where flocks of sheep and goats were feeding.

The dew was still on the grass, and the air was so fresh and sweet in this higher altitude that Joel walked on with a feeling of strength and vigor unknown to him before.

"Oh, look!" he cried, clasping his hands in

delight, as a sudden turn brought them to the upper course of the brook whose waters, falling far below, had refreshed them the night before.

The poetry of the Psalms came as naturally to the lips of this beauty-loving little Israelite as the breath he drew.

Now he repeated, in a low, reverent voice, "'The Lord is my shepherd; I shall not want.' Oh, Rabbi Phineas, did you ever know before that there could be such green pastures and still waters?"

The man smiled at the boy's radiant, upturned face. "'Yea, the earth is the Lord's and the fulness thereof,'" he murmured. "We have indeed a goodly heritage."

Hushed into silence by the voice of the hills and the beauty on every side, they walked on till the road turned again.

Just ahead stood a house unusually large for a country district; everything about it bore an air of wealth and comfort.

"Our journey is at an end now," said Phineas. "Yonder lies the house of Nathan ben Obed. He owns all those flocks and herds we have seen in passing this last half hour. It is with him that I have business; and we will tarry with him until after the Sabbath."

They were evidently expected, for a servant came running out to meet them. He opened the gate and conducted them into a shaded court-yard. Here another servant took off their dusty sandals, and gave them water to wash their feet.

They had barely finished, when an old man appeared in the doorway; his long beard and hair were white as the abba he wore.

Phineas would have bowed himself to the ground before him, but the old man prevented it, by hurrying to take both hands in his, and kiss him on each cheek.

"Peace be to thee, thou son of my good friend Jesse!" he said. "Thou art indeed most welcome."

Joel lagged behind. He was always sensitive about meeting strangers; but the man's cordial welcome soon put him at his ease.

He was left to himself a great deal during the few days following. The business on which the old man had summoned Phineas required long consultations.

One day they rode away together to some outlying pastures, and were gone until night-fall. Joel did not miss them. He was spending long happy hours in the country sunshine. There was something to entertain him, every way he turned. For a while he amused himself by sitting in the door and poring over a roll of parchment that Sarah, the wife of Nathan ben Obed, brought him to read.

She was an old woman, but one would have found it hard to think so, had he seen how briskly she went about her duties of caring for such a large household.

After Joel had read for some little time, he became aware that some one was singing outside, in a whining, monotonous way, and he laid down his book to listen. The voice was not loud, but so penetrating he could not shut it out, and fix his mind on his story again. So he rolled up the parchment and laid it on the chest from which it had been taken; then winding his handkerchief around his head, turban fashion, he limped out in the direction of the voice.

Just around the corner of the house, under a great oak-tree, a woman sat churning. From three smooth poles joined at the top to form a tripod, a goat-skin bag hung by long leather straps. This was filled with cream; she was slapping it violently back and forth in time to her weird song.

Her feet were bare, and she wore only a

coarse cotton dress. But a gay red handkerchief covered her black hair, and heavy copper rings hung from her nose and ears.

The song stopped suddenly as she saw Joel. Then recognizing her master's guest, she smiled at him so broadly that he could see her pretty white teeth.

Joel hardly knew what to say at this unexpected encounter, but bethought himself to ask the way to the sheep-folds and the watch-tower. "It is a long way there," said the woman, doubtfully; Joel flushed as he felt her black eyes scanning his misshapen form.

Just then Sarah appeared in the door, and the maid repeated the question to her mistress.

"To be sure," she said. "You must go out and see our shepherds with their flocks. We have a great many employed just now, on all the surrounding hills. Rhoda, call your son, and bid him bring hither the donkey that he always drives to market."

The woman left her churning, and presently came back with a boy about Joel's age, leading a donkey with only one ear.

Joel knew what that meant. At some time in its life the poor beast had strayed into some neighbor's field, and the owner of the field had been at liberty to cut off an ear in punishment.

The boy that led him wore a long shirt of rough hair-cloth. His feet and legs were brown and tanned. A shock of reddish sunburned hair was the only covering for his head. There was a squint in one eye, and his face was freckled.

He made an awkward obeisance to his mistress.

"Buz," she said, "this young lad is your master's guest. Take him out and show him the flocks and herds, and the sheep-folds. He has never seen anything of shepherd life, so be careful to do his pleasure. Stay!" she added to Joel. "You will not have time to visit them all before the mid-day meal, so I will give you a lunch, and you can enjoy an entire day in the fields."

As the two boys started down the hill, Joel stole a glance at his companion. "What a stupid-looking fellow!" he thought; "I doubt if he knows anything more than this sleepy beast I am riding. I wonder if he enjoys any of this beautiful world around him. How glad I am that I am not in his place."

Buz, trudging along in the dust, glanced at the little cripple on the donkey's back with an inward shiver.

"What a dreadful lot his must be," he thought. "How glad I am that I am not like he is!"

It was not very long till the shyness began to wear off, and Joel found that the stupid shepherd lad had a very busy brain under his shock of tangled hair. His eyes might squint, but they knew just where to look in the bushes for the little hedge-sparrow's nest. They could take unerring aim, too, when he sent the smooth sling-stones whizzing from the sling he carried.

"How far can you shoot with it?" asked Joel.

For answer Buz looked all around for some object on which to try his skill; then he pointed to a hawk slowly circling overhead. Joel watched him fit a smooth pebble into his sling; he had no thought that the boy could touch it at such a distance. The stone whizzed through the air like a bullet, and the bird dropped several yards ahead of them.

"See!" said Buz, as he ran to pick it up, and display it proudly. "I struck it in the head."

Joel looked at him with increasing respect. "That must have been the kind of sling that King David killed the giant with," he said, handing it back after a careful examination.

"King David!" repeated Buz, dully, "seems to

me I have heard of him, sometime or other; but I don't know about the giant."

"Why where have you been all your life?" cried Joel, in amazement. "I thought everybody knew about that. Did you never go to a synagogue?"

Buz shook his bushy head. "They don't have synagogues in these parts. The master calls us in and reads to us on the Sabbath; but I always get sleepy when I sit right still, and so I generally get behind somebody and go to sleep. The shepherds talk to each other a good deal about such things, I am never with them though. I spend all my time running errands."

Shocked at such ignorance, Joel began to tell the shepherd king's life with such eloquence that Buz stopped short in the road to listen.

Seeing this the donkey stood still also, wagged its one ear, and went to sleep. But Buz listened, wider awake than he had ever been before in his life.

The story was a favorite one with Joel, and he put his whole soul into it.

"Who told you that?" asked Buz, taking a long breath when the interesting tale was finished.

"Why I read it myself!" answered Joel.

"Oh, can you read?" asked Buz, looking at Joel in much the same way that Joel had looked at him after he killed the hawk. "I do not see how anybody can. It puzzles me how people can look at all those crooked black marks and call them rivers and flocks and things. I looked one time, just where Master had been reading about a great battle. And I did n't see a single thing that looked like a warrior or a sword or a battle-axe, though he called them all by name. There were several little round marks that might have been meant for sling-stones; but it was more than I could make out, how he could get any sense out of it."

Joel leaned back and laughed till the hills rang, laughed till the tears stood in his eyes, and the donkey waked up and ambled on.

Buz did not seem to be in the least disturbed by his merriment, although he was puzzled as to its cause. He only stooped to pick up more stones for his sling as they went on.

It was not long till they came to some of the men, — great brawny fellows dressed in skins, with coarse matted hair and tanned faces. How little they knew of what was going on in the busy world outside their fields! As Joel talked to them he found that Cæsar's conquests and

Hero's murders had only come to them as vague rumors. All the petty wars and political turmoils were unknown to them. They could talk to him only of their flocks and their faith, both as simple as their lives.

Joel, in his wisdom learned of the Rabbis, felt himself infinitely their superior, child though he was. But he enjoyed his day spent with them. He and Buz ate the ample lunch they had brought, dipped up water from the brook in cups they made of oak-leaves, and both finally fell asleep to the droning music of the shepherd's pipes, played softly on the uplands.

A distant rumble of thunder aroused them, late in the afternoon; and they started up to find the shepherds calling in their flocks. The gaunt sheep dogs raced to and fro, bringing the straying goats together. The shepherds brought the sheep into line with well-aimed sling-shots, touching them first on one side, and then on the other, as oxen are guided by the touch of the goad.

Joel looked up at the darkening sky with alarm. "Who would have thought of a storm on such a day!" he exclaimed.

Buz cocked his eyes at the horizon. "I thought it might come to this," he said; "for as we came along this morning there were no spider-webs on the grass; the ants had not uncovered the doors of their hills; and all the signs pointed to wet weather. I thought though, that the time of the latter rains had passed a week ago. I am always glad when the stormy season is over. This one is going to be a hard one."

"What shall we do?" asked Joel.

Buz scratched his head. Then he looked at Joel. "You never could get home on that trifling donkey before it overtakes us; and they'll be worried about you. I'd best take you up to the sheep-fold. You can stay all night there, very comfortably. I'll run home and tell them where you are, and come back for you in the morning."

Joel hesitated, appalled at spending the night among such dirty men; but the heavy boom of thunder, steadily rolling nearer, silenced his half-spoken objection. By the time the donkey had carried him up the hillside to the stone-walled enclosure round the watch-tower, the shepherds were at the gates with their flocks.

Joel watched them go through the narrow passage, one by one. Each man kept count of his own sheep, and drove them under the rough sheds put up for their protection.

A good-sized hut was built against the hillside,

where the shepherds might find refuge. Buz pointed it out to Joel; then he turned the donkey into one of the sheds, and started homeward on the run.

Joel shuddered as a blinding flash of lightning was followed by a crash of thunder that shook the hut. The wind bore down through the trees like some savage spirit, shrieking and moaning as it flew. Joel heard a shout, and looked out to the opposite hillside. Buz was flying along in break-neck race with the storm. At that rate he would soon be home. How he seemed to enjoy the race, as his strong limbs carried him lightly as a bird soars!

At the top he turned to look back and laugh and wave his arms, — a sinewy little figure standing out in bold relief against a brazen sky.

Joel watched till he was out of sight. Then, as the wind swooped down from the mountains, great drops of rain began to splash through the leaves.

The men crowded into the hut. One of them started forward to close the door, but stopped suddenly, with his brown hairy hand uplifted.

"Hark ye!" he exclaimed.

Joel heard only the shivering of the wind in the tree-tops; but the man's trained ear caught the bleating of a stray lamb, far off and very faint.

"I was afraid I was mistaken in my count; they jostled through the gate so fast I could not be sure." Going to a row of pegs along the wall, he took down a lantern hanging there and lit it; then wrapping his coat of skins more closely around him, and calling one of the dogs, he set out into the gathering darkness.

Joel watched the fitful gleam of the lantern, flickering on unsteadily as a will-o'-the-wisp. A moment later he heard the man's deep voice calling tenderly to the lost animal; then the storm struck with such fury that they had to stand with their backs against the door of the hut to keep it closed.

Flash after flash of lightning blinded them. The wind roared down the mountain and beat against the house till Joel held his breath in terror. It was midnight before it stopped. Joel thought of the poor shepherd out on the hills, and shuddered. Even the men seemed uneasy about him, as hour after hour passed, and he did not come.

Finally he fell asleep in the corner, on a pile of woolly skins. In the gray dawn he was awakened by a great shout. He got up, and went to the door. There stood the shepherd. His bare limbs were cut by stones and torn by thorns. Blood streamed from his forehead where he had been wounded by a falling branch. The mud on his rough garments showed how often he had slipped and fallen on the steep paths.

Joel noticed, with a thrill of sympathy, how painfully he limped. But there on the bowed shoulders was the lamb he had wandered so far to find; and as the welcoming shout arose again, Joel's weak little cheer joined gladly in.

"How brave and strong he is," thought the boy. "He risked his life for just one pitiful little lamb."

The child's heart went strangely out to this rough fellow who stood holding the shivering animal, sublimely unconscious that he had done anything more than a simple duty.

Joel, who felt uncommonly hungry after his supperless night, thought he would mount the donkey and start back alone. But just as he was about to do so, a familiar bushy head showed itself in the door of the sheepfold. Buz had brought him some wheat-cakes and cheese to eat on the way back.

Joel was so busy with this welcome meal that he did not talk much. Buz kept eying him in silence, as if he longed to ask some question. At last, when the cheese had entirely disappeared, he found courage to ask it.

"Were you always like that?" he said abruptly, motioning to Joel's back and leg. Somehow the reference did not wound him as it generally did. He began to tell Buz about the Samaritan boy who had crippled him. He never was able to tell the story of his wrongs without growing passionately angry. He had worked himself into a white heat by the time he had finished.

"I'd get even with him," said Buz, excitedly, with a wicked squint of his eyes.

"How would you do it?" demanded Joel. "Cripple him as he did me?"

"Worse than that!" exclaimed Buz, stopping to take deliberate aim at a leaf overhead, and shooting a hole exactly through the centre with his sling. "I'd blind him as quick as that! It's a great deal worse to be blind than lame."

Joel closed his eyes, and rode on a few moments in darkness. Then he opened them and gave a quick glad look around the landscape. "My! What if I never could have opened them again," he thought. "Yes, Buz, you're right," he said aloud. "It *is* worse to be blind; so I shall take Rehum's eyesight also, some time. Oh, if that time were only here!"

Although the subject of the miracle at Cana had been constantly in the mind of Phineas, and often near his lips, he did not speak of it to his host until the evening before his departure.

It was just at the close of the evening meal. Nathan ben Obed rose half-way from his seat in astonishment, then sank back.

"How old a man is this friend of yours?" he asked.

"About thirty, I think," answered Phineas. "He is a little younger than I."

"Where was he born?"

"In Bethlehem, I have heard it said, though his home has always been in Nazareth."

"Strange, strange!" muttered the man, stroking his long white beard thoughtfully.

Joel reached over and touched Phineas on the arm. "Will you not tell Rabbi Nathan about the wonderful star that was seen at that time?" he asked, in a low tone.

"What was that?" asked the old man, arousing from his reverie.

When Phineas had repeated his conversation with the stranger on the day of his journey, Nathan ben Obed exchanged meaning glances with his wife.

"Send for the old shepherd Heber," he said. "I would have speech with him."

Rhoda came in to light the lamps. He bade her roll a cushioned couch that was in one corner to the centre of the room.

"This old shepherd Heber was born in Bethlehem," he said; "but since his sons and grandsons have been in my employ, he has come north to live. He used to help keep the flocks that belonged to the Temple, and that were used for sacrifices. His has always been one of the purest of lives; and I have never known such faith as he has. He is over a hundred years old, so must have been quite aged at the time of the event of which he will tell us."

Presently an old, old man tottered into the room, leaning on the shoulders of his two stalwart grandsons. They placed him gently on the cushions of the couch, and then went into the court-yard to await his readiness to return. Like the men Joel had seen the day before, they were dressed in skins, and were wild-looking and rough. But this aged father, with dim eyes and trembling wrinkled hands, sat before them like some hoary patriarch, in a fine linen mantle.

Pleased as a child, he saluted his new audience, and began to tell them his only story.

As the years had gone by, one by one the lights of memory had gone out in darkness. Well-known scenes had grown dim; old faces were forgotten; names he knew as well as his own, could not be recalled: but this one story was as fresh and real to him, as on the night he learned it.

The words he chose were simple, the voice was tremulous with weakness; but he spoke with a dramatic fervor that made Joel creep nearer and nearer, until he knelt, unknowing, at the old man's knee, spell-bound by the wonderful tale.

"We were keeping watch in the fields by night," began the old shepherd, "I and my sons and my brethren. It was still and cold, and we spoke but little to each other. Suddenly over all the hills and plains shone a great light,— brighter than light of moon or stars or sunshine. It was so heavenly white we knew it must be the glory of the Lord we looked upon and we were sore afraid, and hid our faces, falling to the ground. And, lo! an angel overhead spake to us from out of the midst of the glory, saying, 'Fear not: for, behold, I bring you good tidings of great joy, which shall be to all people. For unto you is born this day in the city of David a Saviour, which is Christ the Lord. And this shall be a sign unto you; Ye shall find the babe wrapped in swaddling clothes, lying in a manger.'

"And suddenly there was with the angel a multitude of the heavenly host praising God, and saying, 'Glory to God in the highest, peace on earth, good-will toward men!'

"Oh, the sound of the rejoicing that filled that upper air! Ever since in my heart have I carried that foretaste of heaven!"

The old shepherd paused, with such a light on his upturned face that he seemed to his awe-struck listeners to be hearing again that same angelic chorus,— the chorus that rang down from the watch-towers of heaven, across earth's lowly sheep-fold, on that first Christmas night.

There was a solemn hush. Then he said, "And when they were gone away, and the light and the song were no more with us, we spake one to another, and rose in haste and went to Bethlehem. And we found the Babe lying in a manger with Mary its mother; and we fell down and worshipped Him.

"Thirty years has it been since the birth of Israel's Messiah; and I sit and wonder all the day,— wonder when He will appear once more to His people. Surely the time must be well nigh here when He may claim His kingdom. O Lord, let not Thy servant depart until these eyes that beheld the Child shall have seen the King in His beauty!"

Joel remained kneeling beside old Heber, perfectly motionless. He was fitting together the links that he had lately found. A child, heralded by angels, proclaimed by a star worshipped by the Magi! A man changing water into wine at only a word!

"I shall yet see Him!" exclaimed the voice of old Heber, with such sublime assurance of faith that it found a response in every heart.

There was another solemn stillness, so deep that the soft fluttering of a night-moth around the lamp startled them.

Then the child's voice rang out, eager and shrill, but triumphant as if inspired: "Rabbi Phineas, *He* it was who changed the water into wine! — This friend of Nazareth and the babe of Bethlehem are the same!"

The heart of the carpenter was strangely stirred, but it was full of doubt. Not that the Christ had been born, — the teachings of all his lifetime led him to expect that; but that the chosen One could be a friend of his, — the thought was too wonderful for him.

The old shepherd sat on the couch, feebly

twisting his fingers, and talking to himself. He was repeating bits of the story he had just told them: "And, lo, an angel overhead!" he muttered. Then he looked up, whispering softly, "Glory to God in the highest — and peace, yes, on earth peace!"

"He seems to have forgotten everything else," said Nathan, signalling to the men outside to lead him home. "His mind is wiped away entirely, that it may keep unspotted the record of that night's revelation. He tells it over and over, whether he has a listener or not."

They led him gently out, the white-haired, white-souled old shepherd Heber. It seemed to Joel that the wrinkled face was illuminated by some inner light, not of this world, and that he lingered among men only to repeat to them, over and over, his one story. That strange sweet story of Bethlehem's first Christmas-tide.

CHAPTER IV.

EXT morning a goodly train set out from the gates of Nathan ben Obed. It was near the time of the feast of the Passover, and he, with many of his household, was going down to Jerusalem.

The family and guests went first on mules and asses. Behind them followed a train of servants, driving the lambs, goats, and oxen to be offered as sacrifices in the temple, or sold in Jerusalem to other pilgrims.

All along the highway, workmen were busy repairing the bridges, and cleaning the springs and wells, soon to be used by the throngs of travellers.

All the tombs near the great thoroughfares were being freshly white-washed; they gleamed with a dazzling purity through the green trees, only to warn passers-by of the defilement within. For had those on their way to the feast approached too near these homes of the dead, even unconsciously, they would have been accounted unclean, and unfit to partake of the Passover. Nothing escaped Joel's quick sight, from the tulips and marigolds flaming in the fields, to the bright-eyed little viper crawling along the stone-wall.

But while he looked, he never lost a word that passed between his friend Phineas and their host. The pride of an ancient nation took possession of him as he listened to the prophecies they quoted.

Every one they met along the way coming from Capernaum had something to say about this new prophet who had arisen in Galilee. When they reached the gate of the city, a great disappointment awaited them. *He had been there, and gone again.*

Nathan ben Obed and his train tarried only one night in the place, and then pressed on again towards Jerusalem. Phineas went with them.

"You shall go with us next year," he said to Joel; "then you will be over twelve. I shall take my own little ones too, and their mother."

"Only one more year," exclaimed Joel, joyfully. "If that passes as quickly as the one just gone, it will soon be here."

"Look after my little family," said the carpenter, at parting. "Come every day to the work, if you wish, just as when I am here; and remember, my lad, you are almost a man."

Almost a man! The words rang in the boy's thoughts all day as he pounded and cut, keeping time to the swinging motion of hammer and saw. Almost a man! But what kind of one? Crippled and maimed, shorn of the strength that should have been his pride, beggared of his priestly birthright.

Almost, it might be, but never in its fulness, could he hope to attain the proud stature of a perfect man.

A fiercer hate sprang up for the enemy who had made him what he was; and the wild burning for revenge filled him so he could not work. He put away his tools, and went up the narrow outside stairway that led to the flat roof of the carpenter's house. It was called the "upper chamber." Here a latticed pavilion, thickly overgrown with vines, made a cool green retreat where he might rest and think undisturbed.

Sitting there, he could see the flash of white sails on the blue lake, and slow-moving masses of fleecy clouds in the blue of the sky above. They brought before him the picture of the flocks feeding on the pastures of Nathan ben Obed.

Then, naturally enough, there flashed through his mind a thought of Buz. He seemed to see him squinting his little eyes to take aim at a leaf overhead. He heard the stone whirr through it, as Buz said: "I'd blind him!"

Some very impossible plans crept into Joel's day-dreams just then. He imagined himself sitting in a high seat, wrapped in robes of state; soldiers stood around him to carry out his slightest wish. The door would open and Rehum would be brought forth in fetters.

"What is your will concerning the prisoner, O most gracious sovereign," the jailer would ask.

Joel closed his eyes, and waved his hand before an imaginary audience. "Away with him, — to the torture! Wrench his limbs on the rack! Brand his eyelids with hot irons! Let him suffer all that man can suffer and live! Thus shall it be done unto the man on whom the king delighteth to take vengeance!"

Joel was childish enough to take a real satisfaction in this scene he conjured up. But as it faded away, he was man enough to realize it could never come to pass, save in his imagination; he could never be in such a position for revenge, unless, —

That moment a possible way seemed to open for him. Phineas would probably see his friend of Nazareth at the Passover. What could be more natural than that the old friendship should be renewed. He whose hand had changed the water into wine should finally cast out the alien king who usurped the throne of Israel, for one in whose veins the blood of David ran royal red, — what was more to be expected than that?

The Messiah would come to His kingdom, and then — and then — the thought leaped to its last daring limit.

Phineas, who had been His earliest friend and playfellow, would he not be lifted to the right hand of power? Through him, then, lay the royal road to revenge.

The thought lifted him unconsciously to his feet. He stood with his arms out-stretched in the direction of the far-away Temple, like some young prophet. David's cry of triumph rose to his lips: "Thou hast girded me with strength unto the battle," he murmured. "Thou hast also given me the necks of mine enemies, that I might destroy them that hate me!"

A sweet baby voice at the foot of the steps brought him suddenly down from the height of his intense feeling.

"Joel! Joel!" called little Ruth, "where is you?"

Then Jesse's voice added, "We're all a-coming up for you to tell us a story."

Up the stairs they swarmed to the roof, the carpenter's children and half-a-dozen of their little playmates.

Joel, with his head still in the clouds, told them of a mighty king who was coming to slay all other kings, and change all tears — the waters of affliction — into the red wine of joy.

"H'm! I don't think much of that story," said Jesse, with out-spoken candor. "I'd rather hear about Goliath, or the bears that ate up the forty children."

But Joel was in no mood for such stories, just then. On some slight pretext he escaped from his exacting audience, and went down to the sea-shore. Here, skipping stones across the water, or writing idly in the sand, he was free to go on with his fascinating day-dreams.

For the next two weeks the boy gave up work entirely. He haunted the toll-gates and public streets, hoping to hear some startling news from Jerusalem. He was so full of the thought that some great revolution was about to take place, that he could not understand how people could be so indifferent. All on fire with the belief that this man of Nazareth was the one in whom lay the nation's hope, he looked and longed for the return of Phineas, that he might learn more of Him.

But Phineas had little to tell when he came back. He had met his friend twice in Jerusalem,— the same gentle quiet man he had always known, making no claims, working no wonders. Phineas had heard of His driving the money-changers out of the Temple one day, and those who sold doves in its sacred courts, although he had not witnessed the scene.

The carpenter was rather surprised that He should have made such a public disturbance.

"Rabbi Phineas," said Joel, with a trembling voice, "don't you think your friend is the prophet we are expecting?"

Phineas shook his head. "No, my lad, I am sure of it now."

"But the herald angels and the star," insisted the boy.

"They must have proclaimed some one else. He is the best man I ever knew; but there is no more of the king in His nature, than there is in mine."

The man's positive answer seemed to shatter

Joel's last hope. Downcast and disappointed, he went back to his work. Only with money could he accomplish his life's object, and only by incessant work could he earn the shining shekels that he needed.

Phineas wondered sometimes at the dogged persistance with which the child stuck to his task, in spite of his tired, aching body.

He had learned to make sandal-wood jewel-boxes, and fancifully wrought cups to hold the various dyes and cosmetics used by the ladies of the court.

Several times, during the following months, he begged a sail in some of the fishing-boats that landed at the town of Tiberias. Having gained the favor of the keeper of the gates, by various little gifts of his own manufacture, he always found a ready admittance to the palace.

To the ladies of the court, the sums they paid for his pretty wares seemed trifling; but to Joel the small bag of coin hidden in the folds of his clothes was a little fortune, daily growing larger.

CHAPTER V.

IT was Sabbath morning in the house of Laban the Pharisee. Joel, sitting alone in the court-yard, could hear his aunt talking to the smaller children, as she made them ready to take with her to the synagogue.

From the upper chamber on the roof, came also a sound of voices, for two guests had arrived the day before, and were talking earnestly with their host. Joel already knew the object of their visit.

They had been there before, when the preaching of John Baptist had drawn such great crowds from all the cities to the banks of the Jordan. They had been sent out then by the authorities in Jerusalem to see what manner of man was this who, clothed in skins and living in the wilderness, could draw the people so wonderfully, and arouse such intense excitement. Now they had come on a like errand, although on their own authority.

Another prophet had arisen whom this John Baptist had declared to be greater than himself. They had seen Him drive the money-changers from the Temple; they had heard many wild rumors concerning Him. So they followed Him to His home in the little village of Nazareth, where they heard Him talk in the synagogue.

They had seen the listening crowd grow amazed at the eloquence of His teaching, and then indignant that one so humble as a carpenter's son should claim that Isaiah's prophecies had been fulfilled in Himself.

They had seen Him driven from the home of His boyhood, and now had come to Capernaum that they might be witnesses in case this impostor tried to lead these people astray by repeating His claims.

All this Joel heard, and more, as the earnest voices came distinctly down to him through the deep hush of the Sabbath stillness. It shook his faith somewhat, even in the goodness of this friend of his friend Phineas, that these two learned doctors of the Law should consider Him an impostor.

He stood aside respectfully for them to pass, as they came down the outside stairway, and crossed the court-yard on their way to the morning service.

Their long, flowing, white robes, their broad phylacteries, their dignified bearing, impressed him greatly. He knew they were wise, good men whose only aim in life was to keep the letter of the Law, down to its smallest details. He followed them through the streets until they came to the synagogue. They gave no greeting to any one they passed, but walked with reverently bowed heads that their pious meditation might not be disturbed by the outside world. His aunt had already gone by the way of the back streets, as it was customary for women to go, her face closely veiled.

The synagogue, of finely chiselled limestone, with its double rows of great marble pillars, stood in its white splendor, the pride of the town. It had been built by the commander of the garrison who, though a Roman centurion, was a believer in the God of the Hebrews, and greatly loved by the whole people.

Joel glanced up at the lintel over the door, where Aaron's rod and a pot of manna carved in the stone were constant reminders to the daily worshippers of the Hand that fed and guided them from generation to generation.

Joel limped slowly to his place in the congregation. In the seats of honor, facing it, sat his uncle and his guests, among the rulers of the synagogue.

For a moment his eyes wandered curiously around, hoping for a glimpse of the man whose fame was beginning to spread all over Galilee. It had been rumored that He would be there. But Joel saw only familiar faces. The elders took their seats.

During the reading of the usual psalm, the reciting of a benediction, and even the confession of the creed, Joel's thoughts wandered. When the reader took up his scroll to read the passages from Deuteronomy, the boy stole one more quick glance all around. But as the whole congregation arose, and turned facing the east, he resolutely fixed his mind on the duties of the hour.

The eighteen benedictions, or prayers, were recited in silence by each devout worshipper. Then the leader repeated them aloud, all the congregation responding with their deep Amen! and Amen! Joel always liked that part of the service and the chanting that followed.

Another roll of parchment was brought out. The boy looked up with interest. Probably one of his uncle's guests would be invited to read from it, and speak to the people.

No, it was a stranger whom he had not noticed before, sitting behind one of the tall elders, who was thus honored.

Joel's heart beat so fast that the blood throbbed against his ear-drums, as he heard the name called. It was the friend of his friend Phineas, *the Rabbi Jesus.*

Joel bent forward, all his soul in his eyes, as the stranger unrolled the book, and began to read from the Prophets. The words were old familiar ones; he even knew them by heart. But never before had they carried with them such music, such meaning. When He laid aside the roll, and began to speak, every fibre in the boy's being thrilled in response to the wonderful eloquence of that voice and teaching.

The whole congregation sat spell-bound, forgetful of everything except the earnestness of the speaker who moved and swayed them as the wind does the waving wheat.

Suddenly there arose a wild shriek, a sort of demon-like howl that transfixed them with its piercing horror. Every one turned to see the cause of the startling sound. There, near the door, stood a man whom they all knew, — an unhappy creature said to be possessed of an unclean spirit.

"Ha!" he cried, in a blood-curdling tone. "What have we to do with Thee, Jesus of Nazareth? Art thou come to destroy us? I know Thee, who thou art, the holy One of God!"

There was a great stir, especially in the woman's gallery; and those standing nearest him backed away as far as possible.

Every face was curious and excited, at this sudden interruption, — every face but one; the Rabbi Jesus alone was calm.

"Hold thy peace and come out of him!" He commanded. There was one more shriek, worse than before, as the man fell at His feet in a convulsion; but in a moment he stood up again, quiet and perfectly sane. The wild look was gone from his eyes. Whatever had been the strange spell that had bound him before, he was now absolutely free.

There was another stir in the woman's gallery. Contrary to all rule or custom, an aged woman pushed her way out. Down the stairs she went, unveiled through the ranks of the men, to reach her son whom she had just seen restored to reason. With a glad cry she fell forward, fainting, in his arms, and was borne away to the little home, now no longer darkened by the shadow of a sore affliction.

Little else was talked about that day, until the rumor of another miracle began to spread through the town. Phineas, stopping at Laban's house on his way home from an afternoon service, confirmed the truth of it.

One of his neighbors had been dangerously ill with a fever that was common in that part of the country; she was the mother-in-law of Simon bar Jonah. It was at his home that the Rabbi Jesus had been invited to dine.

As soon as He entered the house, they besought Him to heal her. Standing beside her, He rebuked the fever; and immediately she arose, and began to help her daughter prepare for the entertainment of their guest.

"Abigail was there yesterday," said Phineas, "to carry some broth she had made. She thought then it would be impossible for the poor creature to live through the night. I saw the woman a few hours ago, and she is perfectly well and strong."

That night when the sun was setting, and the Sabbath was at an end, a motley crowd streamed along the streets to the door of Simon bar Jonah.

Men carried on couches; children in their mother's arms; those wasted by burning fevers; those shaken by unceasing palsy; the lame; the blind; the death-stricken, — all pressing hopefully on.

What a scene in that little court-yard as the sunset touched the wan faces and smiled into dying eyes. Hope for the hopeless! Balm for the broken in body and spirit! There was rejoicing in nearly every home in Capernaum that night, for none were turned away. Not one was refused. It is written, "He laid His hand on every one of them, and healed them."

That he might not seem behind his guests in zeal and devotion to the Law, the dignified Laban would not follow the crowds.

"Let others be carried away by strange doctrines and false prophets, if they will," he declared; "as for me and my household, we will cling to the true faith of our fathers."

So the three sat in the upper chamber on the roof, and discussed the new teacher with many shakes of their wise heads.

"It is not lawful to heal on the Sabbath day," they declared. "Twice during the past day He has openly transgressed the Law. He will lead all Galilee astray!"

But Galilee cared little how far the path

turned from the narrow faith of the Pharisees, so long as it led to life and healing.

Down in the garden below, the children climbed up on the grape-arbor, and peered through the vines at the surging crowds which they would have joined, had it not been for Laban's strict commands.

One by one they watched people whom they knew go by, some carried on litters, some leaning on the shoulders of friends. One man crawled painfully along on his hands and knees.

After awhile the same people began to come back.

"Look, quick, Joel!" one of the children cried; "there goes Simon ben Levi. Why, his palsy is all gone! He does n't shake a bit now! And there's little Martha that lives out near Aunt Rebecca's! Don't you know how white and thin she looked when they carried her by a little while ago? See! she is running along by herself now as well as we are!"

The children could hardly credit their own sense of sight, when neighbors they had known all their lives to be bed-ridden invalids came back cured, singing and praising God.

It was a sight they never could forget. So they watched wonderingly till darkness fell, and the last happy-hearted healed one had gone home to a rejoicing household.

While the fathers on the roof were deciding they would have naught of this man, the children in the grape-arbor were storing up in their simple little hearts these proofs of his power and kindness.

Then they gathered around Joel on the doorstep, while he repeated the story that the old shepherd Heber had told him, of the angels and the star, and the baby they had worshipped that night in Bethlehem.

"Come, children," called his Aunt Leah, as she lit the lamp that was to burn all night. "Come! It is bed-time!"

His cousin Hannah lingered a moment after the others had gone in, to say, "That was a pretty story, Joel. Why don't you go and ask the good man to straighten your back?"

Strange as it may seem, this was the first time the thought had occurred to him that he might be benefited himself. He had been so long accustomed to thinking of himself as hopelessly lame, that the wonderful cures he had witnessed had awakened no hope for himself. A new life seemed to open up before him at the little girl's question. He sat on the doorstep thinking about it until his Uncle Laban came down and crossly ordered him to go to bed.

He went in, saying softly to himself, " I will go to him to-morrow; yes, early in the morning!"

Strange that an old proverb should cross his mind just then. "Boast not thyself of to-morrow. Thou knowest not what a day may bring forth."

CHAPTER VI.

HEN Joel went out on the streets next morning, although it was quite early, he saw a disappointed crowd coming up from the direction of Simon's house on the lake shore.

"Where have all these people been?" he asked of the baker's boy, whom he ran against at the first corner.

The boy stopped whistling, and rested his basket of freshly baked bread against his knee, as he answered: —

"They were looking for the Rabbi who healed so many people last night. Say! do you know," he added quickly, as if the news were too good to keep, "he healed my mother last night. You cannot think how different it seems at home, to have her going about strong and well like she used to be."

Joel's eyes brightened. "Do you think he'll do anything for me, if I go to him now?" he asked wistfully. "Do you suppose he could straighten out such a crooked back as mine?

Look how much shorter this leg is than the other. Oh, *do* you think he could make them all right?"

The boy gave him a critical survey, and then answered, emphatically, "Yes! It really does not look like it would be as hard to straighten you as old Jeremy, the tailor's father. He was twisted all out of shape, you know. Well, I'll declare! There he goes now!"

Joel looked across the street. The wrinkled face of the old basket-weaver was a familiar sight in the market; but Joel could hardly recognize the once crippled form, now restored to its original shapeliness.

"I am going right now," he declared, starting to run in his excitement. "I can't wait another minute."

"But he's gone!" the boy called after him. "That's why the people are all coming back."

Joel sat down suddenly on a ledge projecting from the stone-wall. "Gone!" he echoed drearily. It was as if he had been starving, and the life-giving food held to his famished lips had been suddenly snatched away. Both his heart and his feet felt like lead when he got up after awhile, and dragged himself slowly along to the carpenter's house.

It was such a bitter disappointment to be so near the touch of healing, and then to miss it altogether.

No cheerful tap of the hammer greeted him. The idle tools lay on the deserted workbench. "Disappointed again!" he thought. Then the doves cooed, and he caught a glimpse of Ruth's fair hair down among the garden lilies.

"Where is your father, little one?" he called.

"Gone away wiv 'e good man 'at makes everybody well," she answered. Then she came skipping down the path to stand close beside him, and say confidentially: "I saw Him — 'e good man — going by to Simon's house. I peeped out 'tween 'e wose-vines, and He looked wite into my eyes wiv His eyes, and I could n't help loving Him!"

Joel looked into the beautiful baby face, thinking what a picture it must have made, as framed in roses it smiled out on the Tender-hearted One, going on His mission of help and healing.

With her little hand in his, she led him back to hope, for she took him to her mother, who comforted him with the assurance that Phineas expected to be home soon, and doubtless his friend would be with him.

So there came another time to work by him-

"'I PEEPED OUT 'TWEEN 'E WOSE-VINES'"

self and dream of the hour surely dawning. And the dreams were doubly sweet now; for side by side with his hope of revenge, was the belief in his possible cure.

They heard only once from the absent ones. Word came back that a leper had been healed. Joel heard it first, down at the custom-house. He had gotten into the way of strolling down in that direction after his work was done; for here the many trading-vessels from across the lake, or those that shipped from Capernaum, had to stop and pay duty. Here, too, the great road of Eastern commerce passed which led from Damascus to the harbors of the West. So here he would find a constant stream of travellers, bringing the latest news from the outside world.

The boy did not know, as he limped up and down the water's edge, longing for some word from his absent friends, that near by was one who watched almost as eagerly as himself.

It was Levi-Matthew, one of the officials, sitting in the seat of custom. Sprung from the same priestly tribe as Joel, he had sunk so low, in accepting the office of tax-gatherer, that the righteous Laban would not have touched him so much as with the tip of his sandal.

"Bears and lions," said a proverb, "might be the fiercest wild beasts in the forests; but publicans and informers were the worst in cities."

One could not bear witness in the courts, and the disgrace extended to the whole family. They were even classed with robbers and murderers. No doubt there was deep cause for such a feeling; as a class they were unscrupulous and unjust. There might have been good ones among their number, but the company they kept condemned them to the scorn of high and low.

When a Jew hates, or a Jew scorns, be sure it is thoroughly done; there is no half-way course for his intense nature to take.

So this son of Levi, sitting in the seat of custom, and this son of Levi strolling past him, were, socially, as far apart as the east is from the west, — as unlike as thorn and blossom on the same tribal stem.

Matthew knew all the fishermen and ship-owners that thronged the busy beach in front of him. The sons of Jonah and of Zebedee passed him daily; and he must have wondered when he saw them throw down their nets and leave everything to follow a stranger.

He must have wondered also at the reports on every tongue, and the sights he had seen himself of miraculous healing. But while strangely drawn towards this new teacher from Nazareth, it could have been with no thought that the hand and the voice were for him. He was a publican, and how could they reach to such depths?

A caravan had just stopped. The pack-animals were being unloaded, bales and packages opened, private letters pried into. The insolent officials were tossing things right and left, as they made a list of the taxable goods.

Joel was watching them with as much interest as if he had not witnessed such scenes dozens of times before, till he noticed a group gathering around one of the drivers. He was telling what he had seen on his way to Capernaum. Several noisy companions kept interrupting him to bear witness to the truth of his statements.

"And he who but a moment before had been the most miserable of lepers stood up before us all, cleansed of his leprosy. His skin was soft and fair as a child's, and his features were restored to him," said the driver.

Joel and Levi-Matthew stood side by side. At another time the boy might have drawn his clothes away to keep from brushing against the despised tax-gatherer. But he never noticed now that their elbows touched.

When he had heard all there was to be told, he limped away to carry the news to Abigail. To know that others were being cured daily made him all the more impatient for the return of this friend of Phineas.

The publican turned again to his pen and his account-book. He, too, looked forward with a burning heart to the return of the Nazarene, unknowing why he did so.

At last Joel heard of the return, in a very unexpected way. There were guests in the house of Laban again. One of the rabbis who had been there before, and a scribe from Jerusalem. Now there were longer conferences in the upper chamber, and graver shakings of the head, over this false prophet whose fame was spreading wider.

The miracle of healing the paralytic at the pool of Bethesda, when he had gone down to Jerusalem to one of the many feasts, had stirred Judea to its farthest borders. So these two men had been sent to investigate.

On the very afternoon of their arrival, a report flew through the streets that the Rabbi Jesus was once more in the town. Their host led them with all the haste their dignity would allow, to the house where He was said to be preaching.

The common people fell back when they saw them, and allowed them to pass into the centre of the throng.

The Rabbi stood in the doorway, so that both those in the house and without could distinctly hear Him. The scribe had never seen Him before, and in spite of his deep-seated prejudice could not help admiring the man whom he had come prepared to despise. It was no wild fanatic who stood before him, no noisy debater whose fiery eloquence would be likely to excite and inflame His hearers.

He saw a man of gentlest dignity; truth looked out from the depths of His calm eyes. Every word, every gesture, carried with it the conviction that He who spoke taught with God-given authority.

The scribe began to grow uneasy as he listened, carried along by the earnest tones of the speaker.

There was a great commotion on the edge of the crowd, as some one tried to push through to the centre.

"Stand back! Go away!" demanded angry voices.

The scribe was a tall man, and by stretching a little, managed to see over the heads of the others. Four men, bearing a helpless paralytic, were trying to carry him through the throngs; but they would not make room for this interruption.

After vainly hunting for some opening through which they might press, the men mounted the steep, narrow staircase on the outside of the building, and drew the man up, hammock and all, to the flat roof on which they stood.

There was a sound of scraping and scratching as they broke away the brush and mortar that formed the frail covering of the roof. Then the people in the room below saw slowly coming down upon them between the rafters, this man whom no obstacle could keep back from the Great Physician.

But the paralyzed hands could not lift themselves in supplication; the helpless tongue could frame no word of pleading, — only the eyes of the sick man could look up into the pitying face bent over him, and implore a blessing.

The scribe leaned forward, confidently expecting to hear the man bidden to arise. To his surprise and horror, the words he heard were: "Son, thy *sins* be forgiven thee!"

He looked at Laban and his companion, and the three exchanged meaning glances. When they looked again at the speaker, His eyes seemed to read their inmost thoughts.

"Wherefore think ye evil in your hearts?" He asked, with startling distinctness. "Whether is it easier to say to the sick of the palsy, Thy sins be forgiven thee; or to say, Arise, and take up thy bed, and walk? But that ye may know that the Son of man hath power on earth to forgive sins," here He turned to the helpless form lying at His feet, "I say unto thee, Arise, and take up thy bed, and go thy way unto thine house."

The man bounded to his feet, and picking up the heavy rug on which he had been lying, went running and leaping out of their midst.

Without a word, Laban and his two guests drew their clothes carefully around them, and picked their way through the crowd. Phineas, who stood at the gate, gave them a respectful greeting. Laban only turned his eyes away with a scowl, and passed coldly on.

"The man is a liar and a blasphemer!" exclaimed the scribe, as they sat once more in the privacy of Laban's garden.

"Only God can forgive sins!" added his companion. "This paralytic should have taken a sin-offering to the priest. For only by the blood of sacrifice can one hope to obtain pardon."

"Still He healed him," spoke up the scribe, musingly.

"Only through the power of Satan!" interrupted Laban. "When He says He can forgive sins, He blasphemes."

The other Pharisee leaned forward to say, in an impressive whisper: "Then you know the Law on that point. He should be stoned to death, His body hung on a tree, and then buried with shame!"

It was not long after that Joel, just back from a trip to Tiberias in a little sailing-boat, came into the garden. He had been away since early morning, so had heard nothing of what had just occurred; he had had good luck in disposing of his wares, and was feeling unusually cheerful. Hearing voices in the corner of the garden, he was about to pass out again, when his uncle called him sternly to come to him at once.

Surprised at the command, he obeyed, and was questioned and cross-questioned by all three. It was very little he could tell them about his friend's plans; but he acknowleged proudly that Phineas had always known this famous man from Nazareth, even in childhood, and was one of his most devoted followers.

"This man Phineas is a traitor to the faith!" roared Laban. "He is a dangerous man, and in league with these fellows to do great evil to our nation."

The scribe and the rabbi nodded approvingly.

"Hear me, now!" he cried, sternly. "Never again are you to set foot over his threshold, or have any communication whatsoever with him or his associates. I make no idle threat; if you disobey me in this, you will have cause to wish you had never been born. You may leave us now!"

Too surprised and frightened to say a word, the child slipped away. To give up his daily visit to the carpenter's house, was to give up all that made his life tolerable; while to be denied even speaking to his associates, meant to abandon all hope of cure.

But he dared not rebel; obedience to those in authority was too thoroughly taught in those days to be lightly disregarded. But his uncle seemed to fear that his harsh command would be eluded in some way, and kept such a strict watch over him, that he rarely got beyond the borders of the garden by himself.

One day he was all alone in the grape-arbor, looking out into the streets that he longed to be in, since their freedom had been denied him.

A little girl passed, carrying one child in her

arms, and talking to another who clung to her skirts. It was Jerusha.

Joel threw a green grape at her to attract her attention, and then beckoned her mysteriously to come nearer. She set the baby on the ground, and gave him her bracelet to play with, while she listened to a whispered account of his wrongs through the latticed arbor.

"It's a shame!" she declared indignantly. "I'll go right down to the carpenter's house and tell them why you cannot go there any more. And I'll keep watch on all that happens, and let you know. I go past here every day, and if I have any news, I'll toss a pebble over the wall and cluck like a hen. Then if nobody is watching, you can come to this hole in the arbor again."

The next day, as Joel was going in great haste to the baker's, whither his aunt had sent him, he heard some one behind him calling him to wait. In another moment Jerusha was in speaking distance, nearly bent double with the weight of her little brother, whom she was carrying as usual.

"There!" she said, with a puff of relief, as she put him on his own feet. "Wait till I get my breath! It's no easy thing to carry such a load and run at the same time! How did you get out?"

"There was an errand to be done, and no one else to do it," answered Joel, "so Aunt sent me."

"Oh, I've got such news for you!" she exclaimed. "Guess what has happened! Your Rabbi Jesus has asked Levi-Matthew to be one of His followers, and go around with Him wherever He goes. Think of it! One of those horrid tax-gatherers! He settled his accounts and gave up his position in the custom-house yesterday. And he is getting ready for a great feast. I heard the butcher and the wine-dealer both telling about the big orders he had given them.

"All the publicans and low common people that are his friends are invited. Yes, and so is your friend the carpenter. Think of that, now! He is going to sit down and eat with such people! Of course respectable folks will never have anything more to do with him after that! I guess your uncle was right about him, after all!"

Both the little girl's face and manner expressed intense disgust.

Joel was shocked. "Oh, are you sure?" he cried. "You certainly must be mistaken! It cannot be so!"

"I guess I know what I see with my own eyes, and hear with my own ears!" she retorted, angrily.

"My father says they are a bad lot. People that go with publicans are just as unclean themselves. If you know so much more than everybody else, I'll not trouble myself to run after you with any more news. Mistaken, indeed!"

With her head held high, and her nose scornfully turned up, she jerked her little brother past him, and went quickly around the corner of the street.

The indignation of some of the rabbis knew no bounds. "It has turned out just as I predicted," said the scribe to Laban, at supper. "They are nothing but a set of gluttons and wine-bibbers!"

There was nothing else talked of during the entire meal. How Joel's blood boiled as he listened to their conversation! The food seemed to choke him. As they applied one coarse epithet after another to his friend Phineas, all the kindness and care this man had ever given him seemed to rise up before him. But when they turned on the Nazarene, all the stories Joel had heard in the carpenter's house of His gentle sinless childhood, all the tokens he had seen himself of His pure unselfish manhood, seemed to cry out against such gross injustice.

It was no light thing for a child to contradict

the doctors of the Law, and, in a case of this kind, little less than a crime to take the stand Joel did.

But the memory of two faces gave him courage: that of Phineas as it had looked on him through all those busy happy hours in the carpenter's home; the other face he had seen but once, that day of healing in the synagogue, — who, having once looked into the purity of those eyes, the infinite tenderness of that face, could sit calmly by and raise no voice against the calumny of his enemies?

The little cripple was white to the lips, and he trembled from head to foot as he stood up to speak.

The scribe lifted up both hands, and turned to Laban with a meaning shrug of the shoulders. " To think of finding such heresy in your own household!" he exclaimed. "Among your own children!"

"He is no child of mine!" retorted Laban. "Nor shall he stay among them!" Then he turned to Joel.

"Boy, take back every word you have just uttered! Swear you will renounce this man, — this son of perdition, — and never have aught to say well of Him again!"

Joel looked around the table, at each face that shone out pale and excited in the yellow lamplight. His eyes were dilated with fear; his heart thumped so in the awful pause that followed, that he thought everybody else must hear it.

"I cannot!" he said hoarsely. "Oh, I cannot!"

"Then take yourself out of my sight forever. The doors of this house shall never open for you again!"

There was a storm of abuse from the angry man at this open defiance of his authority. With these two cold, stern men to nod approval at his zealousness, he went to greater lengths than he might otherwise have done.

With one more frightened glance around the table, the child hurried out of the room. The door into the street creaked after him, and Joel limped out into the night, with his uncle's curse ringing in his ears.

CHAPTER VII.

HINEAS, going along the beach that night, in the early moonlight, towards his home, saw a little figure crouched in the shadow of a low building beside the wharf. It was shaking with violent sobs. He went up to the child, and took its hands down from its wet face, with a comforting expression of pity. Then he started back in surprise. It was Joel!

"Why, my child! My poor child!" he exclaimed, putting his arm around the trembling, misshapen form. "What is the meaning of all this?"

"Uncle Laban has driven me away from home!" sobbed the boy. "He was angry because you and Rabbi Jesus were invited to Levi-Matthew's feast. He says I have denied the faith, and am worse than an infidel. He says I am fit only to be cast out with the dogs and publicans! — and — and —" he ended with a wail. "Oh, he sent me away with his curse!"

Phineas drew him closer, and stroked the head on his shoulder in pitying silence.

"Fatherless and motherless and lame!" the boy sobbed bitterly. "And now, a homeless outcast, blighted by a curse, I have been sitting here with my feet in the dark water, thinking how easy it would be to slip down into it and forget; but, Rabbi Phineas, that face will not let me, — that face of your friend, — I keep seeing it all the time!"

Phineas gathered the boy so close in his arms that Joel could feel his strong, even heart-beats.

"My child," he said solemnly, "call me no more, Rabbi! Henceforth, it is to be *father* Phineas. You shall be to me as my own son!"

"But the curse!" sobbed Joel. "The curse that is set upon me! It will blight you too!"

"Nay," was the quiet answer; "for it is written, 'As the bird by wandering, as the swallow by flying, *so the curse, causeless, shall not come.*'"

But the boy still shook as with a chill. His face and hands were burning hot.

"Come!" said Phineas. He picked him up in his strong arms, and carried him down the beach to Abigail's motherly care and comforting.

"He will be a long time getting over the

shock of this," she said to her husband, when he was at last soothed to sleep.

"Ah, loyal little heart!" he answered, "he has suffered much for the sake of his friendship with us!"

Poor little storm-tossed bark! In the days that followed he had reason to bless the boisterous winds, that blew him to such a safe and happy harbor!

Over on the horns of Mount Hattin, the spring morning began to shine. The light crept slowly down the side of the old mountain, till it fell on a little group of men talking earnestly together. It was the Preacher of Galilee, who had just chosen twelve men from among those who followed Him to help Him in His ministry.

They gathered around Him in the fresh mountain dawn, as He pictured the life in store for them. Strange they did not quail before it, and turn back disheartened. Nay, not strange! For in the weeks they had been with Him, they had learned to love Him so, that His "follow me," that drew them from the toll-gate and fishing-boat, was stronger than ties of home and kindred.

Just about this time, Phineas and Joel were starting out from Capernaum to the mountain.

Hundreds of people were already on the way; people who had come from all parts of Judea, and beyond the Jordan. Clouds of dust rose above the highway as the travellers trudged along.

Joel was obliged to walk slowly, so that by the time they reached the plain below, a great multitude had gathered.

"Let's get close," he whispered. He had heard that those who barely touched the garments of the strange Rabbi were made whole, and it was with the hope that he might steal up and touch Him unobserved that he had begged Phineas to take him on such a long, painful walk.

"There is too great a crowd, now," answered Phineas. "Let us rest here awhile, and listen. Let me lift you up on this big rock, so that you can see. 'Sh! He is speaking!"

Joel looked up, and, for the second time in his life, listened to words that thrilled him like a trumpet call, — words that through eighteen hundred years have not ceased to vibrate; with what mighty power they must have fallen when, for the first time, they broke the morning stillness of those mountain wilds!

Joel forgot the press of people about him, forgot even where he was, as sentence after sentence seemed to lift him out of himself, till he could catch glimpses of lofty living such as he had never even dreamed of before.

Round by round, he seemed to be carried up some high ladder of thought by that voice, away from all that was common and low and earthly, to a summit of infinite love and light.

Still the voice led on, "Ye have heard that it hath been said, 'An eye for an eye and a tooth for a tooth.'"

Joel started so violently at hearing his own familiar motto, that he nearly lost his balance on the rock.

"But I say unto you That you resist not evil: but whosoever shall smite thee on thy right cheek, turn to him the other also. . . . Ye have heard that it hath been said, Thou shalt love thy neighbor, and hate thine enemy. But I say unto you, Love your enemies, bless them that curse you, do good to them that hate you, and pray for them which despitefully use you, and persecute you."

Poor little Joel, it was a hard doctrine for him to accept! How could he give up his hope of revenge, when it had grown with his growth till it had come to be as dear as life itself?

He heard little of the rest of the sermon, for through it all the words kept echoing, "Bless them that curse you! Do good to them that hate you! Pray for them which despitefully use you!"

"Oh, I can't! I can't!" he groaned inwardly.

"I have found a chance for you to ride home," said Phineas, when the sermon was over, and the people began to file down the narrow mountain paths. "But there will be time for you to go to Him first, for healing. You have only to ask, you know."

Joel took an eager step forward, and then shrank back guiltily. "Not now," he murmured, "some other time." He could not look into those clear eyes and ask a blessing, when he knew his heart was black with hate.

After all his weeks of waiting the opportunity had come; but he dared not let the Sinless One look into his soul.

Phineas began an exclamation of surprise, but was interrupted by some one asking him a question. Joel took advantage of this to climb up behind the man who had offered him a ride. All the way home he weighed the two desires in his mind, — the hope of healing, and the hope of revenge.

By the time the two guardian fig-trees were in sight, he had decided. He would rather go helpless and halting through life than give up his cherished purpose.

But there was no sleep for him that night, after he had gone up to his little chamber on the roof. He seemed to see that pleading face on the mountain-side; it came to him again and again, with the words, "Bless them that curse you! Pray for them that despitefully use you!"

All night he fought against yielding to it. Time and again he turned over on his bed, and closed his eyes; but it would not let him alone.

He thought of Jacob wrestling with the angel till day-break, and knew in his heart that the sweet spirit of forgiveness striving with his selfish nature was some heavenly impulse from another world.

At last when the cock-crowing commenced at dawn, and the stars were beginning to fade, he drew up his crooked little body, and knelt with his face to the kindling east.

"Father in heaven," he prayed softly, "bless mine enemy Rehum, and forgive all my sins, — fully and freely as I now forgive the wrong he has done to me."

A feeling of light-heartedness and peace, such as he had never known before, stole over him. He could not settle himself to sleep, though worn out with his night's long vigil.

Hastily slipping on his clothes, he tiptoed down the stairs, and limped, bare-headed, down to the beach. The lake shimmered and glowed under the faint rose and gray of the sky like a deep opal. The early breeze blew the hair back from his pale face with a refreshing coolness.

It seemed to him the world had never looked one half so beautiful before, as he stood there.

A firm tread on the gravel made him turn partly around. A man was coming up the beach; it was the friend of Phineas. As if drawn by some uncontrollable impulse, Joel started to meet Him, an unspoken prayer in his pleading little face.

Not a word was said. For one little instant Joel stood there by the shining sea, his hand held close in the loving hand of the world's Redeemer. For one little instant he looked up into His face; then the man passed on.

Joel covered his face with his hands, seeming to hear the still small voice that spoke to the prophet out of the whirlwind.

"He is the Christ!" he whispered reverently, — "He is the Christ!"

In his exalted feeling all thought of a cure had left him; but as he walked on down the beach, he noticed that he no longer limped. He was moving along with strong, quick strides. He

"NOT A WORD WAS SAID"

shook himself and threw back his shoulders; there was no pain in the movement. He passed his hands over his back and down his limbs.

Oh, he was straight and strong and sinewy! He seemed a stranger to himself, as running and leaping, then stopping to look down and feel his limbs again, he ran madly on.

Suddenly he cast his garments aside and dived into the lake. Before his injury, he had been able to swim like a fish, now he reached out with long powerful strokes that sent him darting through the cold water with a wonderful sense of exhilaration.

Then he dressed again, and went on running and leaping and climbing till he was exhausted, and his first wild delirious joy began to subside into a deep quiet thankfulness. Then he went home, radiant in the happiness of his new-found cure.

But more than the mystery of the miracle, more than the joy of the healing, was the remembrance of that moment, that one little moment, when he felt the clasp of the Master's hand, and seemed wrapped about with the boundless love of God.

From that moment, he lived but to serve and to follow Him.

CHAPTER VIII.

HIGH up among the black lava crags of Perea stood the dismal fortress of Macherus. Behind its close prison bars a restless captive groped his way back and forth in a dungeon cell. Sometimes, at long intervals, he was given such liberty as a chained eagle might have, when he was led up into one of the towers of the gloomy keep, and allowed to look down, down into the bottomless gorges surrounding it. For months he had chafed in the darkness of his underground dungeon; escape was impossible.

It was John Baptist, brought from the wild, free life of the desert to the tortures of the "Black Castle." Here he lay at the mercy of Herod Antipas, and death might strike at any moment. More than once, the whimsical monarch had sent for him, as he sat at his banquets, to be the sport of the passing hour.

The lights, the color, the flash of gems may have dazzled his eyes for a brief space, accustomed as they were to the midnight darkness of his cell; but his keen vision saw, under the paint and purple of royal apparel, the corrupt life of king and court.

Pointing his stern, accusing finger at the uneasy king, he cried, "It is not lawful for thee to have thy brother's wife!" With words that stung like hurtling arrows, he laid bare the blackened, beastly life that sought to hide its foulness under royal ermine.

Antipas cowered before him; and while he would gladly have been freed from a man who had such power over him, he dared not lift a finger against the fearless, unflinching Baptist.

But the guilty Herodias bided her time, with blood-thirsty impatience; his life should pay the penalty of his bold speech.

Meanwhile he waited in his cell, with nothing but memories to relieve the tediousness of the long hours. Over and over again he lived those scenes of his strange life in the desert, — those days of his preparation, — the preaching to the multitudes, the baptizing at the ford of the Jordan.

He wondered if his words still lived; if any

of his followers still believed on him. But more than all, he wondered what had become of that One on whom he had seen the spirit of God descending out of heaven in the form of a dove.

"Where art Thou now?" he cried. "If Thou art the Messiah, why dost Thou not set up Thy kingdom, and speedily give Thy servant his liberty?" The empty room rang often with that cry; but the hollow echo of his own words was the only answer.

One day the door of his cell creaked back far enough to admit two men, and then shut again, leaving them in total darkness. In that momentary flash of light, he recognized two old followers of his, Timeus bar Joram and Benjamin the potter.

With a cry of joy he groped his way toward them, and clung to their friendly hands.

"How did you manage to penetrate these Roman-guarded walls?" he asked, in astonishment.

"I knew the warden," answered Benjamin. "A piece of silver conveniently closes his eyes to many things. But we must hasten! Our time is limited."

They had much to tell of the outside world. Pilate had just given special offence, by appropriating part of the treasure of the Temple, derived from the Temple tax, to defray the cost of great conduits he had begun, with which to supply Jerusalem with water.

Stirred up by the priests and rabbis, the people besieged the government house, crying loudly that the works be given up. Armed with clubs, numbers of soldiers in plain clothes surrounded the great mob, and killed so many of the people that the wildest excitement prevailed throughout all Judea and Galilee.

There was a cry for a national uprising to avenge the murder.

"They only need a leader!" exclaimed John. "Where is He for whom I was but a voice crying in the wilderness? Why does He not show Himself?"

"We have just come from the village of Nain," said Timeus bar Joram. "We saw Him stop a funeral procession and raise a widow's son to life. He was followed by a motley throng whom He had healed of all sorts of diseases; and there were twelve men whom He had chosen as life-long companions.

"We questioned some of them closely, and they gave us marvellous reports of the things He had done."

"Is it not strange," asked Benjamin the potter, " that having such power He still delays to establish His kingdom ? "

The captive prophet made no answer for awhile. Then he groped in the thick darkness till his hand rested heavily on Benjamin's arm.

"Go back, and say that John Baptist asks, 'Art Thou the Coming One, or must we look for another?'"

Days passed before the devoted friends found themselves once more inside the prison walls. They had had a weary journey over rough hills and rocky by-paths.

"What did He say?" demanded the prisoner, eagerly.

"Go and tell John what ye saw and heard: that the blind receive sight; the lame walk; the lepers are cleansed; the deaf hear; the dead are raised; and the poor have the gospel preached unto them."

The man stood up, his long hair hanging to his shoulder, his hand uplifted, and his eyes dilated like a startled deer that has caught the sound of a coming step.

"The fulfilment of the words of Isaiah!" he cried. "For he hath said, ' Your God will come and save you. Then the eyes of the blind shall be opened, and the ears of the deaf shall be unstopped. Then shall the lame man leap as a hart, and the tongue of the dumb sing!' Yea, he *hath* bound up the broken-hearted; and he shall yet 'proclaim liberty to the captives, and the opening of the prison to them that are bound, to proclaim the acceptable year of the Lord!'"

Then with both hands clasped high above his head, he made the prison ring with the cry, "The kingdom is at hand! The kingdom is at hand! I shall soon be free!"

Not long after that, the castle blazed with the lights of another banquet. The faint aroma of wines, mingled with the heavy odor of countless flowers, could not penetrate the grim prison walls. Nor could the gay snatches of song and the revelry of the feast. No sound of applause reached the prisoner's ear, when the daughter of Herodias danced before the king.

Sitting in darkness while the birthday banqueters held high carnival, he heard the heavy tramp of soldiers' feet coming down the stairs to his dungeon. The great bolts shot back, the rusty hinges turned, and a lantern flickered its light in his face, as he stood up to receive his executioners.

A little while later his severed head was taken on a charger to the smiling dancing girl. She stifled a shriek when she saw it; but the wicked Herodias looked at it with a gleam of triumph in her treacherous black eyes.

When the lights were out, and the feasters gone, two men came in at the warden's bidding, — two men with heavy hearts, and voices that shook a little when they spoke to each other. They were Timeus and Benjamin. Silently they lifted the body of their beloved master, and carried it away for burial; and if a tear or two found an unaccustomed path down their bearded cheeks, no one knew it, under cover of the darkness.

So, out of the Black Castle of Macherus, out of the prison-house of a mortal body, the white-souled prophet of the wilderness went forth at last into liberty.

For him, the kingdom was indeed at hand.

Meanwhile in the upper country, Phineas was following his friend from village to village. He had dropped his old familiar form of address, so much was he impressed by the mysterious power he saw constantly displayed.

Now when he spoke of the man who had been

both friend and playfellow, it was almost reverently that he gave Him the title of Master.

It was with a heavy heart that Joel watched them go away. He, too, longed to follow; but he knew that unless he took the place at the bench, Phineas could not be free to go.

Gratitude held him to his post. No, not gratitude alone; he was learning the Master's own spirit of loving self-sacrifice. As he dropped the plumb-line over his work, he measured himself by that perfect life, and tried to straighten himself to its unbending standard.

He had his reward in the look of pleasure that he saw on the carpenter's face when Phineas came in, unexpectedly, one day, dusty and travel-stained.

"How much you have accomplished!" he said in surprise. "You have filled my place like a grown man."

Joel stretched his strong arms with a slight laugh. "It is a pleasure to work now," he said. "It seems so queer never to have a pain, or that worn-out feeling of weakness that used to be always with me. At first I was often afraid it was all a happy dream, and could not last. I am getting used to it now. Where is the Master?" Joel asked, as Phineas turned towards the house.

"He is the guest of Simon. He will be here some days, my son. I know you wish to be with Him as much as possible, so I shall not expect your help as long as He stays."

"If I could only do something for Him!" Was Joel's constant thought during the next few days. Once he took a coin from the little money bag that held his hoarded savings — a coin that was to have helped buy his revenge — and bought the ripest, juiciest pear he could find in the market. Often he brought Him water, fresh and cold from the well when He looked tired and warm from His unceasing work.

Wherever the Master turned, there, close beside Him, was a beaming little face, so full of love and childish sympathy that it must have brought more refreshment to His thirsty soul than either the choice fruit or the cooling water.

One evening after a busy day, when He had talked for hours to the people on the seashore who had gathered around the boat in which He sat, He sent away the multitude.

"Let us pass over unto the other side," He said.

Joel slipped up to Andrew, who was busily arranging their sails. "Let me go, too!" he whispered pleadingly.

"Well," assented the man, carelessly, "You can make yourself useful, I suppose. Will you hand me that rope?"

Joel sprang to obey. Presently the boat pushed away from the shore, and the town, with its tumult and its twinkling lights, was soon left far behind.

The sea was like glass, so calm and unruffled that every star above could look down and see its unbroken reflection in the dark water below.

Joel, in the hinder part of the ship, lay back in his seat with a sigh of perfect enjoyment. The smooth gliding motion of the boat rested him; the soft splash of the water soothed his excited brain. He had seen his Uncle Laban that afternoon among other of the scribes and Pharisees, and heard him declare that Beelzebub alone was responsible for the wonders they witnessed.

Joel's indignation flared up again at the memory. He looked down at the Master, who had fallen asleep on a pillow, and wondered how anybody could possibly believe such evil things about Him.

It was cooler out where they were now. He wondered if he ought not to lay some covering over the sleeping form. He took off the outer mantle that he wore, and bent forward to lay it over the Master's feet. But he drew back timidly, afraid of wakening Him. "I'll wait awhile," he said to himself, folding the garment across his knees in readiness.

Several times he reached forward to lay it over Him, and each time drew back. Then he fell asleep himself.

From its situation in the basin of the hills, the Galilee is subject to sudden and furious storms. The winds, rushing down the heights, meet and clash above the water, till the waves run up like walls, then sink again into seething whirlpools of danger.

Joel, falling asleep in a dead calm, awoke to find the ship rolling and tossing and half-full of water. The lightning's track was followed so closely by the crash of thunder, there was not even pause enough between to take one terrified gasp.

Still the Master slept. Joel, drenched to the skin, clung to the boat's side, expecting that every minute would be his last. It was so dark and wild and awful! How helpless they were, buffetted about in the fury of the storm!

As wave after wave beat in, some of the men could no longer control their fear.

"Master!" they called to the sleeping man, as they bent over Him in terror. "Carest Thou not that we perish?"

He heard the cry for help. The storm could not waken Him from His deep sleep of exhaustion, but at the first despairing human voice, He was up, ready to help.

Looking up at the midnight blackness of the sky, and down at the wild waste of waters, He stretched out His hand.

"*Peace!*" he commanded in a deep voice. "*Be still!*" The storm sank to earth as suddenly as a death-stricken raven; a great calm spread over the face of the waters. The silent stars shone out in their places; the silent sea mirrored back their glory at His feet.

The men huddled fearfully together. "What manner of man is this?" they asked, one of another. "Even the wind and the sea obey Him!"

Joel, looking up at the majestic form, standing so quietly by the railing, thought of the voice that once rang out over the night of Creation with the command, "Let there be light!" At its mere bidding light had flowed in across the darkness of primeval night.

Just so had this voice thrilled the storm with its "Peace! Be still!" into utter calm.

The child crouched at His feet, burying his face in his mantle, and whispering, in awe and adoration, "He *is* the Christ! He is the son of God!"

CHAPTER IX.

AFTER that night of the voyage to the Gadarenes, Joel ceased to be surprised at the miracles he daily witnessed. Even when the little daughter of Jairus, the ruler of the synagogue, was called back to life, it did not seem so wonderful to him as the stilling of the tempest.

Many a night after Phineas had gone away again with the Master to other cities, Joel used to go down to the beach, and stand looking across the water as he recalled that scene.

The lake had always been an interesting place to him at night. He liked to watch the fishermen as they flashed their blazing torches this way and that. A sympathetic thrill ran through him as they sighted their prey, and raised their bare sinewy arms to fling the net or fly the spear.

But after that morning of healing, and that night of tempest, it seemed to be a sacred place, to be visited only on still nights, when the town slept, and heaven bent nearer in the starlight to the quiet earth.

The time of the Passover was drawing near, — the time that Joel had been looking forward to since Phineas had promised him a year ago that he should go to Jerusalem.

The twelve disciples who had been sent out to all the little towns through Galilee, to teach the things they had themselves been taught, and work miracles in the name of Him who had sent them, began to come slowly back. They had an encouraging report to bring of their work; but it was shadowed by the news they had heard of the murder of John Baptist.

Joel joined them as soon as they came into Capernaum, and walked beside Phineas as the footsore travellers pressed on a little farther towards Simon's house.

"When are we going to start for Jerusalem?" was his first eager question.

Phineas looked searchingly into his face as he replied, "Would you be greatly disappointed, my son, not to go this year?"

Joel looked perplexed; it was such an unheard of thing for Phineas to miss going up to the Feast of the Passover.

"These are evil times, my Joel," he explained.

"John Baptist has just been beheaded. The Master has many enemies among those in high places. It would be like walking into a lion's den for Him to go up to Jerusalem.

"Even here He is not safe from the hatred of Antipas, and after a little rest will pass over into the borders of the tetrarch Philip. We have no wish to leave Him!"

"Oh, why should He be persecuted so?" asked Joel, looking with tear-dimmed eyes at the man walking in advance of them, and talking in low earnest tones to John, who walked beside Him.

"You have been with Him so much, father Phineas. Have *you* ever known Him to do anything to make these men His enemies?"

"Yes," said Phineas. "He has drawn the people after Him until they are jealous of His popularity. He upsets their old traditions, and teaches a religion that ignores some of the Laws of Moses. I can easily see why they hate Him so. They see Him at such a long distance from themselves, they can not understand Him. Healing on the Sabbath, eating with publicans and sinners, disregarding the little customs and ceremonies that in all ages have set apart our people as a chosen race, are crimes in their eyes.

"If they only could get close enough to understand Him; to see that His pure life needs no ceremonies of multiplied hand-washings; that it is His broad love for His fellow-men that makes Him stoop to the lowest classes, — I am sure they could not do otherwise than love Him.

"Blind fanatics! They would put to death the best man that ever lived, because He is so much broader and higher than they that the little measuring line of their narrow creed cannot compass Him!"

"Is He never going to set up His kingdom?" asked Joel. "Does He never talk about it?"

"Yes," said Phineas; "though we are often puzzled by what He says, and ask ourselves His meaning."

They had reached the house by this time, and as Simon led the way to its hospitable door, Phineas said, "Enter with them, my lad, if you wish. I must go on to my little family, but will join you soon."

To Joel's great pleasure, he found they were to cross the lake at once, to the little fishing port of Bethsaida. It was only six miles across.

"We have hardly had time to eat," said Andrew to Joel, as they walked along towards the boat. "I will be glad to get away to some desert place, where we may have rest from the people that are always pushing and clamoring about us."

"How long before you start?" asked Joel.

"In a very few minutes," answered Andrew; "for the boat is in readiness."

Joel glanced from the street above the beach to the water's edge, as if calculating the distance.

"Don't go without me," he said as, breaking into a run, he dashed up the beach at his utmost speed. He was back again in a surprisingly quick time, with a cheap little basket in his hand; he was out of breath with his rapid run.

"Did n't I go fast?" he panted. "I could not have done that a few weeks ago. Oh, it feels so good to be able to run when I please! It is like flying."

He lifted the cover of the basket. "See!" he said. "I thought the Master might be hungry; but I had no time to get anything better. I had to stop at the first stall I came to."

At the same time the boat went gliding out into the water with its restful motion, thousands of people were pouring out of the villages on foot, and hurrying on around the lake, ahead of them.

The boat passed up a narrow winding creek, away from the sail-dotted lake; its green banks seemed to promise the longed-for quiet and rest. But there in front of them waited the crowds they had come so far to avoid.

They had brought their sick for healing. They needed to be helped and taught; they were "as sheep without a shepherd!" He could not refuse them.

Joel found no chance to offer the food he had bought so hastily with another of his hoarded coins, — the coins that were to have purchased his revenge.

As the day wore on, he heard the disciples ask that the multitudes might be sent away.

"It would take two hundred pennyworth of bread to feed them," said Philip, "and even that would not be enough."

Andrew glanced over the great crowds and stroked his beard thoughtfully. "There is a lad here which hath five barley loaves and two small fishes, but what are they among so many?"

Joel hurried forward and held out his basket with its little store, — five flat round loaves of bread, not much more than one hungry man could eat, and two dried fishes.

He hardly knew what to expect as the people were made to sit down on the grass in orderly ranks of fifties.

His eyes grew round with astonishment as the Master took the bread, gave thanks, and then passed it to the disciples, who, in turn, distributed it among the people. Then the two little fishes were handed around in the same way.

Joel turned to Phineas, who had joined them some time ago. "Do you see that?" he asked excitedly. "They have been multiplied a thousand fold!"

Phineas smiled. "We drop one tiny grain of wheat into the earth," he said, "and when it grows and spreads and bears dozens of other grains on its single stalk, we are not astonished. When the Master but does in an instant, what Nature takes months to do, we cry, 'a miracle!' 'Men are more wont to be astonished at the sun's eclipse, than at its daily rising,'" he quoted, remembering his conversation with the old traveller, on his way to Nathan ben Obed's.

A feeling of exaltation seized the people as they ate the mysterious bread; it seemed that the days of miraculous manna had come again. By the time they had all satisfied their hunger, and twelve basketfuls of the fragments had been gathered up, they were ready to make Him their king. The restlessness of the times had taken possession of them; the burning excitement must find vent in some way, and with one accord they demanded Him as their leader.

Joel wondered why He should refuse. Surely no other man he had ever known could have resisted such an appeal.

The perplexed fisherman, at Jesus's command, turned their boat homeward without Him. To their simple minds it seemed that He had made a mistake in resisting the homage forced upon Him by the people; they longed for the time to come when they should be recognized as the honored officials in the new kingdom. Many a dream of future power and magnificence must have come to them in the still watches of the night, as they drifted home in the white light of the Passover moon.

Many a time in the weeks that followed, Joel slipped away to his favorite spot on the beech, a flat rock half hidden by a clump of oleander bushes. Here, with his feet idly dangling in the ripples, he looked out over the water, and recalled the scenes he had witnessed there.

It seemed so marvellous to him that the

Master could have ever walked on those shining waves; and yet he had seen Him that night after the feeding of the multitudes. He had seen, with his own frightened eyes, the Master walk calmly towards the boat across the unsteady water, and catch up the sinking Peter, who had jumped overboard to meet Him. It grieved and fretted the boy that this man, of God-given power and such sweet unselfish spirit, could be so persistently misunderstood by the people. He could think of nothing else.

He had not been with the crowds that pressed into the synagogue the Sabbath after the thousands had been fed; but Phineas came home with grim lips and knitted brows, and told him about it.

"The Master knew they followed Him because of the loaves and fishes," he said. "He told them so.

"When we came out of the door, I could not help looking up at the lintel on which is carved the pot of manna; for when they asked Him for a sign that they might believe Him, saying, 'Our fathers ate manna in the wilderness!' He answered: 'I am the bread of life! Ye have seen me, and yet believe not!'

"While He talked there was a murmuring all

over the house against Him, because He said that He had come down from heaven. Your uncle Laban was there. I heard him say scornfully: 'Is not this the son of Joseph, whose father and mother we know? How doth He now say, "I am come down out of heaven"?' Then he laughed a mocking little laugh, and nudged the man who stood next to him. There are many like him; I could feel a spirit of prejudice and persecution in the very air. Many who have professed to be His friends have turned against Him."

While Phineas was pouring out his anxious forebodings to his wife and Joel, the Master was going homeward with His chosen twelve.

"Would ye also go away?" He asked wistfully of His companions, as He noted the cold, disapproving looks of many who had only the day before been fed by Him, and who now openly turned their backs on Him.

Simon Peter gave a questioning glance into the faces of his companions; then he pressed a step nearer. "Lord, to whom shall we go?" he answered impulsively. "Thou hast the words of eternal life. And we have believed, and know that Thou art the Holy One of God."

The others nodded their assent, all but one. Judas Iscariot clutched the money bags he held, and looked off across the lake, to avoid the searching eyes that were fixed upon him.

These honest Galileans were too simple to suspect others of dark designs, yet they had never felt altogether free with this stranger from Judea. He had never seemed entirely one of them. They did not see in his crafty quiet manners, the sheep's clothing that hid his wolfish nature; but they could feel his lack of sympathetic enthusiasm.

He had been one of those who followed only for the loaves and fishes of a temporal kingdom, and now, in his secret soul, he was sorry he had joined a cause in whose final success he was beginning to lose faith.

The sun went down suddenly that night behind a heavy cloud, as a gathering storm began to lash the Galilee and rock the little boats anchored at the landings.

The year of popularity was at an end.

CHAPTER X.

ABIGAIL sat just inside the door, turning the noisy hand-mill that ground out the next day's supply of flour. The rough mill-stones grated so harshly on each other that she did not hear the steps coming up the path. A shadow falling across the door-way made her look up.

"You are home early, my Phineas," she said, with a smile. "Well, I shall soon have your supper ready. Joel has gone to the market for some honey and — "

"Nay! I have little wish to eat," he interrupted, "but I have much to say to you. Come! the work can wait."

Abigail put the mill aside, and brushing the flour from her hands, sat down on the step beside him, wondering much at his troubled face.

He plunged into his subject abruptly. "The Master is soon going away," he said, "that those in the uttermost parts of Galilee may be taught of Him. And He would fain have others beside the twelve He has chosen to go with Him on His journey."

"And you wish to go too?" she questioned, as he paused.

"Yes! How can I do otherwise? And yet how can I leave you and the little ones alone in these troubled times? You cannot think how great the danger is. Remember how many horrors we have lately heard. The whole country is a smouldering volcano, ready to burst into an eruption at any moment. A leader has only to arise, and all Israel will take up arms against the powers that trample us under foot."

"Is not this prophet, Jesus, He who is to save Israel?" asked Abigail. "Is He not even now making ready to establish His kingdom?"

"I do not understand Him at all!" said Phineas, sadly. "He does talk of a kingdom in which we are all to have a part; but He never seems to be working to establish it. He spends all His time in healing diseases and forgiving penitent sinners, and telling us to love our neighbors.

"Then, again, why should He go down to the beach, and choose for His confidential friends just simple fishermen. They have neither influence nor money. As for the choice of that publican Levi-Matthew, it has brought disgrace on the whole movement. He does not seem to know how to sway the popular feeling. I believe He might have had the support of the foremost men of the nation, if He had approached them differently.

"He shocks them by setting aside laws they would lay down their lives rather than violate. He associates with those they consider unclean; and all His miracles cannot make them forget how boldly He has rebuked them for hypocrisy and unrighteousness. They never will come to His support now; and I do not see how a new government can be formed without their help."

Abigail laid her hand on his, her dark eyes glowing with intense earnestness, as she answered: "What need is there of armies and human hands to help?

"Where were the hosts of Pharaoh when our fathers passed through the Red Sea? Was there bloodshed and fighting there?

"Who battled for us when the walls of Jericho fell down? Whose hand smote the Assyrians at Sennacherib? Is the Lord's arm shortened that He cannot save?

"Why may not His prophet speak peace to

Jerusalem as easily as He did the other night to the stormy sea? Why may not His power be multiplied even as the loaves and fishes?

"Why may not the sins and backslidings of the people be healed as well as Joel's lameness; or the glory of the nation be quickened into a new life, as speedily as He raised the daughter of Jairus?

"Isaiah called Him the Prince of Peace. What are all these lessons, if not to teach us that the purposes of God do not depend on human hands to work out their fulfilment?"

Her low voice thrilled him with its inspiring questions, and he looked down into her rapt face with a feeling of awe.

"Abigail," he said softly, "'my source of joy,' — you are rightly named. You have led me out of the doubts that have been my daily torment. I see now, why He never incites us to rebel against the yoke of Cæsar. In the fulness of time He will free us with a breath.

"How strange it should have fallen to my lot to have been His playmate and companion. My wonder is not that He is the Messiah; but that I should have called Him friend, all these years, unknowing."

"How long do you expect to be away?" she

asked, after a pause, suddenly returning to the first subject.

"Several months, perhaps. There is no telling what insurrections and riots may arise, all through this part of the country. Since the murder of John Baptist, Herod has come back to his court in Tiberias. I dislike to leave you here alone."

Abigail, too, looked grave, and neither spoke for a little while. "I have it!" she exclaimed at length, with a pleased light in her eyes. "I have often wished I could make a long visit in the home of my girlhood. The few days I have spent in my father's house, those few times I have gone with you to the feasts, have been so short and unsatisfactory. Can I not take Joel and the children to Bethany? Neither father nor mother has ever seen little Ruth, and we could be so safe and happy there till your return."

"Why did I not come to you before with my worries?" asked Phineas. "How easily you make the crooked places straight!"

Just then the children came running back from the market. Abigail went into the house with the provisions they had brought, leaving their father to tell them of the coming separation and the long journey they had planned.

A week later, Phineas stood at the city gate,

watching a little company file southward down the highway. He had hired two strong, gayly-caparisoned mules from the owner of the caravan. Abigail rode on one, holding little Ruth in her arms; Joel mounted the other, with Jesse clinging close behind him.

Abigail, thinking of the joyful welcome awaiting her in her old home, and the children happy in the novelty of the journey, set out gayly.

But Phineas, thinking of the dangers by the way, and filled with many forebodings, watched their departure with a heavy heart.

At the top of a little rise in the road, they turned to look back and wave their hands. In a moment more they were out of sight. Then Phineas, grasping his staff more firmly, turned away, and started on foot in the other direction, to follow to the world's end, if need be, the friend who had gone on before.

It was in the midst of the barley harvest. Jesse had never been in the country before. For the first time, Nature spread for him her great picture-book of field and forest and vineyard, while Abigail read to him the stories.

First on one side of the road, then the other, she pointed out some spot and told its history.

Here was Dothan, where Joseph went out to

see his brothers, dressed in his coat of many colors. There was Mount Gilboa, where the arrows of the Philistines wounded Saul, and he fell on his own sword and killed himself. Shiloh, where Hannah brought little Samuel to give him to the Lord; where the Prophet Eli, so old that his eyes were too dim to see, sat by the gate waiting for news from the army, and when word was brought back that his two sons were dead, and the Ark of the Covenant taken, here it was that he fell backward from his seat, and his neck was broken.

All these she told, and many more. Then she pointed to the gleaners in the fields, and told the children to notice how carefully Israel still kept the commandment given so many centuries before: "When ye reap the harvest of your land, thou shalt not wholly reap the corners of thy field, neither shalt thou gather the gleanings of thy harvest. And thou shalt not glean thy vineyard, neither shalt thou gather every grape of thy vineyard, thou shalt leave them for the poor and the stranger."

At Jacob's well, where they stopped to rest, Joel lifted Jesse up, and let him look over the curb. The child almost lost his balance in astonishment, when his own wondering little face looked up at him from the deep well. He backed away from it quickly, and looked carefully into the cup of water Joel handed him, for more than a minute, before he ventured to drink.

The home to which Abigail was going was a wealthy one. Her father, Reuben, was a goldsmith, and for years had been known in Jerusalem not only for the beautifully wrought ornaments and precious stones that he sold in his shop near the Temple, but for his rich gifts to the poor.

"Reuben the Charitable," he was called, and few better deserved the name. His business took him every day to the city; but his home was in the little village of Bethany, two miles away. It was one of the largest in Bethany, and seemed like a palace to the children, when compared to the humble little home in Capernaum.

Joel only looked around with admiring eyes; but Jesse walked about, laying curious little fingers on everything he passed. The bright oriental curtains, the soft cushions and the costly hangings, he smoothed and patted. Even the silver candlesticks and the jewelled cups on the side table were picked up and examined, when his mother happened to have her back turned.

There were no pictures in the house; the Law forbade. But there were several mirrors of bright polished metal, and Jesse never tired of watching his own reflection in them.

Ruth stayed close beside her mother. "She is a ray of God's own sunshine," said her grandmother, as she took her in her arms for the first time. The child, usually afraid of strangers, saw in Rebecca's face a look so like her mother's that she patted the wrinkled cheeks with her soft fingers. From that moment her grandmother was her devoted slave.

Jesse was not long in finding the place he held in his grandfather's heart. The old man, whose sons had all died years before, seemed to centre all his hopes on this son of his only daughter. He kept Jesse with him as much as possible; his happiest hours were when he had the child on his knee, teaching him the prayers and precepts and proverbs that he knew would be a lamp to his feet in later years.

"Nay! do not punish the child!" he said, one morning when Jesse had been guilty of some disobedience. Abigail went on stripping the

"'WE TALKED LATE'"

leaves from an almond switch she just had broken off.

"Why, father," she said, with a smile, "I have often seen you punish my brothers for such disobedience, and have as often heard you say that one of Solomon's wisest sayings is, 'Chasten thy son while there is hope, and let not thy soul spare for his crying.' Jesse misses his father's firm rule, and is getting sadly spoiled."

"That is all true, my daughter," he acknowledged; "still I shall not stay here to witness his punishment."

Abigail used the switch as she had intended. The boy had overheard the conversation, and the cries that reached his grandfather as he rode off to the city were unusually loud and appealing. They may have had something to do with the package the good man carried home that night, — cakes and figs and a gay little turban more befitting a young prince than the son of a carpenter.

"Who lives across the street?" asked Joel, the morning after their arrival.

"Two old friends of mine," answered Abigail. "They came to see me last night as soon as they heard I had arrived. You children were all asleep. We talked late, for they wanted to hear all I could tell them of Rabbi Jesus. He was here last year, and Martha said He and her brother Lazarus became fast friends. Ah, there is Lazarus now! — that young man just coming out of the house. He is a scribe, and goes up to write in one of the rooms of the Temple nearly every day.

"Mary says some of the copies of the Scriptures he has made are the most beautifully written that she has ever seen."

"See!" exclaimed Joel, "he has dropped one of the rolls of parchment he was carrying, and does not know it. I'll run after him with it."

He was hardly yet accustomed to the delight of being so fleet of foot; no halting step now to hinder him. He almost felt as if he were flying, and was by the young man's side nearly as soon as he had started.

"Ah, you are the guest of my good neighbor, Reuben," Lazarus said, after thanking him courteously. "Are you not the lad whose lameness has just been healed by my best friend? My sisters were telling me of it. It must be a strange experience to suddenly find yourself changed from a helpless cripple to such a strong, straight lad as you are now. How did it make you feel?"

"Oh, I can never begin to tell you, Rabbi

Lazarus," answered Joel. "I did not even think of it that moment when He held my hand in His. I only thought how much I loved Him. I had been starving before, but that moment He took the place of everything, — father, mother, the home love I had missed, — and more than that, the love of God seemed to come down and fold me so close and safe, that I knew He was the Messiah. I did not even notice that I was no longer lame, until I was far down the beach. Oh, you do not know how I wanted to follow Him! If I could only have gone with Him instead of coming here!"

"Yes, my boy, I know!" answered the young man, gently; "for I, too, love Him."

This strong bond of sympathy between the two made them feel as if they had known each other always.

"Come walk with me a little way," said Lazarus. "I am going up to Jerusalem to the Temple. Or rather, would you not like to come all the way? I have only to carry these rolls to one of the priests, then I will be at liberty to show you some of the strange sights in the city."

Joel ran back for permission. Only stopping

to wind his white linen turban around his head, he soon regained his new-found friend.

His recollection of Jerusalem was a very dim, confused one. Time and time again he had heard pilgrims returning from the feasts trying to describe their feelings when they had come in sight of the Holy City. Now as they turned with the road, the view that rose before him made him feel how tame their descriptions had been.

The morning sun shone down on the white marble walls of the Temple and the gold that glittered on the courts, as they rose one above the other; tower and turret and pinnacle shot back a dazzling light.

It did not seem possible to Joel that human hands could have wrought such magnificence. He caught his breath, and uttered an exclamation of astonishment.

Lazarus smiled at his pleasure. "Come," he said, "it is still more beautiful inside."

They went very slowly through Solomon's Porch, for every one seemed to know the young man, and many stopped to speak to him. Then they crossed the Court of the Gentiles. It seemed like a market-place; for cages of doves were kept there for sale, and lambs, calves, and oxen bleated and lowed in their stalls till Joel could scarcely hear what his friend was saying, as they pushed their way through the crowd, and stood before the Gate Beautiful that led into the Court of the Women.

Here Lazarus left Joel for a few moments, while he went to give the rolls to the priest for whom he had copied them.

Joel looked around. Then for the first time since his healing, he wondered if it would be possible for him to ever take his place among the Levites, or become a priest as he had been destined.

While he wondered, Lazarus came back and led him into the next court. Here he could look up and see the Holy Place, over which was trained a golden vine, with clusters of grapes as large as a man's body, all of purest gold. Beyond that he knew was a heavy veil of Babylonian tapestry, hyacinth and scarlet and purple, that veiled in awful darkness the Holy of Holies.

As he stood there thinking of the tinkling bells, the silver trumpets, the clouds of incense, and the mighty songs, a great longing came over him to be one of those white-robed priests, serving daily in the Temple.

But with the wish came the recollection of a quiet hillside, where only bird-calls and whirr of wings stirred the stillness; where a breeze from the sparkling lake blew softly through the grass, and one Voice only was heard, proclaiming its glad new gospel under the open sky.

"No." he thought to himself; "I'd rather be with Him than wear the High Priest's mitre."

It was almost sundown when they found themselves on the road homeward. They had visited place after place of interest.

Lazarus found the boy an entertaining companion, and the friendship begun that day grew deep and lasting.

CHAPTER XI.

"WHAT are you looking for, grandfather?" called Jesse, as he pattered up the outside stairs to the roof, where Reuben stood, scanning the sky intently.

"Come here, my son," he called. "Stand right here in front of me, and look just where I point. What do you see?"

The child peered anxiously into the blue depths just now lit up by the sunset.

"Oh, the new moon!" he cried. "Where did it come from?"

"Summer hath dropped her silver sickle there, that Night may go forth to harvest in her starfields," answered the old man. Then seeing the look of inquiry on the boy's face, hastened to add, "Nay, it is the censer that God's hand set swinging in the sky, to remind us to keep the incense of our praises ever rising heavenward. Even now a messenger may be running towards the Temple, to tell the Sanhedrin that it has appeared. Yea, other eyes have been sharper than mine, for see! Already the beacon light has been kindled on the Mount of Olives!"

Jesse watched the great bonfire a few minutes, then ran to call his sister. By the time they were both on the roof, answering fires were blazing on the distant hilltops throughout all Judea, till the whole land was alight with the announcement of the Feast of the New Moon.

"I wish it could be this way every night, don't you, Ruth?" said Jesse. "Are you not glad we are here?"

The old man looked down at the children with a pleased smile. "I'll show you something prettier than this, before long," he said. "Just wait till the Feast of Weeks, when the people all come to bring the first fruits of the harvests. I am glad your visit is in this time of the year, for you can see one festival after another."

The day the celebration of the Feast of Weeks commenced, Reuben left his shop in charge of the attendants, and gave up his entire time to Joel and Jesse.

"We must not miss the processions," he said. "We will go outside the gates a little way, and watch the people come in."

They did not have long to wait till the stream

of people from the upper countries began to pour in; each company carried a banner bearing the name of the town from which it came. A white ox, intended for a peace-offering, was driven first; its horns were gilded, and its body twined with olive wreaths.

Flocks of sheep and oxen for the sacrifice, long strings of asses and camels bearing freewill gifts to the Temple, or old and helpless pilgrims that could not walk, came next.

There were wreaths of roses on the heads of the women and children; bands of lilies were tied around the sheaves of wheat. Piled high in the silver vessels of the rich, or peeping from the willow baskets of the poor, were the choicest fruits of the harvest.

Great bunches of grapes from whose purple globes the bloom had not been brushed, velvety nectarines, tempting pomegranates, mellow pears, juicy melons, — these offerings of fruit and flowers gleamed all down the long line, for no one came empty-handed up this "Hill of the Lord."

As they drew near the gates, a number of white-robed priests from the Temple met them. Reuben lifted Jesse in his arms that he might have a better view. "Listen," he said. Joel climbed up on a large rock.

A joyful sound of flutes commenced, and a mighty chorus went up: "I was glad when they said unto me, let us go into the house of the Lord. Our feet shall stand within thy gates, O Jerusalem!"

Voice after voice took up the old psalm, and Reuben's deep tones joined with the others, as they chanted, "Peace be within thy walls, and prosperity within thy palaces!"

Following the singing pilgrims to the Temple, they saw the priests take the doves that were to be for a burnt-offering, and the first fruits that were to be laid on the altars.

Jesse held fast to his grandfather's hand as they passed through the outer courts of the Temple. He was half frightened by the din of voices, the stamping and bellowing and bleating of the animals as they were driven into the pens.

He had seen one sacrificial service; the great stream of blood pouring over the marble steps of the altar, and the smoke of the burnt-offering were still in his mind. It made him look pityingly now at the gentle-eyed calves and the frightened lambs. He was glad to get away from them.

Soon after the time of this rejoicing was over,

came ten solemn days that to Joel were full of interest and mystery. They were the days of preparation for the Fast of the Atonement. Disputes between neighbors were settled, and sins confessed.

The last great day, the most solemn of all, was the only time in the whole year when the High Priest might draw aside the veil, and enter into the Holy of Holies.

With all his rich robes and jewels laid aside, clad only in simple white, with bare feet and covered head, he had to go four times into the awful Presence. Once to offer incense, once to pray, to sprinkle the blood of a goat towards the mercy-seat, and then to bring out the censer.

That was the day when two goats were taken; by casting lots one was chosen for a sacrifice. On the other the High Priest laid the sins of the people, and it was driven out into the wilderness, to be dashed to pieces from some high cliff.

Tears came into Joel's eyes, as he watched the scape-goat driven away into the dreary desert. He pitied the poor beast doomed to such a death because of his nation's sins.

Then came the closing ceremonies, when the great congregation bowed themselves three times to the ground, with the High Priest shouting solemnly, "Ye are clean! Ye are clean! Ye are clean!"

Joel was glad when the last rite was over, and the people started to their homes, as gay now as they had been serious before.

"When are we going back to our other home?" asked Ruth, one day.

"Why, are you not happy here, little daughter?" said Abigail. "I thought you had forgotten all about the old place."

"I want my white pigeons," she said, with a quivering lip, as if she had suddenly remembered them. "I don't want my father not to be here!" she sobbed; "and I want my white pigeons!"

Abigail picked her up and comforted her. "Wait just a little while. I think father will surely come soon. I will get my embroidery, and you may go with me across the street."

Ruth had been shy at first about going to see her mother's friends; but Martha coaxed her in with honey cakes she baked for that express purpose, and Mary told her stories and taught her little games.

After a while she began to flit in and out of the house as fearlessly as a bright-winged butterfly.

One day her mother was sitting with the sisters in a shady corner of their court-yard, where a climbing honeysuckle made a cool sweet arbor. Ruth was going from one to the other, watching the bright embroidery threads take the shape of flowers under their skilful fingers. Suddenly she heard the faint tinkle of a silver bell. While she stood with one finger on her lip to listen, Lazarus came into the court-yard.

"See what I have brought you, little one," he said. "It is to take the place of the pigeons you are always mourning for."

It was a snow-white lamb, around which he had twined a garland of many colored flowers, and from whose neck hung the little silver bell she had heard.

At first the child was so delighted she could only bury her dimpled fingers in the soft fleece, and look at it in speechless wonder. Then she caught his hand, and left a shy little kiss on it, as she lisped, "Oh, you're so good! You're *so* good!"

After that day Ruth followed Lazarus as the white lamb followed Ruth; and the sisters hardly knew which sounded sweeter in their quiet home, the tinkling of the silver bell, or the happy prattle of the baby voice.

Abigail spent many happy hours with her friends. One day as they sat in the honeysuckle arbor, busily sewing, Ruth and Jesse came running towards them.

"I see my father coming, and another man," cried the boy. "I'm going to meet them."

They all hastened to the door, just as the tired, dusty travellers reached it.

"Peace be to this house, and all who dwell therein," said the stranger, before Phineas could give his wife and friends a warmer greeting.

"We went first to your father's house, but, finding no one at home, came here," said Phineas.

"Come in!" insisted Martha. "You look sorely in need of rest and refreshment."

But they had a message to deliver before they could be persuaded to eat or wash.

"The Master is coming," said Phineas. "He has sent out seventy of His followers, to go by twos into every town, and herald His approach, and proclaim that the day of the Lord is at hand. We have gone even into Samaria to carry the tidings there."

"At last, at last!" cried Mary, clasping her hands. "Oh, to think that I have lived to see this day of Israel's glory!"

"Tell us what the Master has been doing," urged Abigail, after the men had been refreshed by food and water.

First one and then the other told of miracles they had seen, and repeated what He had taught. Even the children crept close to listen, leaning against their father's knees.

"There has been much discussion about the kingdom that is to be formed. While we were in Peter's house in Capernaum, some of the disciples came quarrelling around Him, to ask who should have the highest positions. I suppose those who have followed Him longest think they have claim to the best offices."

"What did He say?" asked Abigail, eagerly.

Phineas laid his hand on Ruth's soft curls. "He took a little child like this, and set it in our midst, and said that he who would be greatest in His kingdom, must become even like unto it!"

"Faith and love and purity on the throne of the Herods," cried Martha. "Ah, only Jehovah can bring such a thing as that to pass!"

"Are you going to stay at home now, father?" asked Jesse, anxiously.

"No, my son. I must go on the morrow to carry my report to the Master, of the reception we have had in every town. But I will soon be back again to the Feast of Tabernacles."

"Carry with you our earnest prayer that the Master will abide with us when He comes again to Bethany," said Martha, as her guests departed. "No one is so welcome in our home, as the friend of our brother Lazarus."

The preparation for the Feast of the Tabernacles had begun. "I am going to take the children to the city with me to-day!" said Reuben, one morning, "to see the big booth I am having built. It will hold all our family, and as many friends as may care to share it with us."

Jesse was charmed with the great tent of green boughs.

"I wish I could have been one of the children that Moses led up out of Egypt," he said, with a sigh.

"Why, my son?" asked Reuben.

"So's I could have wandered around for forty years, living in a tent like this. How good it smells, and how pretty it is! I wish you and grandmother would live here all the time!"

The next day Phineas joined them. It was a happy family that gathered in the leafy booth for a week of out-door rejoicing in the cool autumn time.

"Where is the Master?" asked Abigail.

"I know not," answered her husband. "He sent us on before."

"Will He be here, I wonder?" she asked, and that question was on nearly every lip in Jerusalem.

"Will He be here?" asked the throngs of pilgrims who had heard of His miracles, and longed to see the man who could do such marvellous things.

"Will He be here?" whispered the scribes to the Pharisees. "Let Him beware!"

"Will He be here?" muttered Caiaphas the High Priest. "Then better one man should die, than that the whole community perish."

The sight that dazzled the eyes of the children that first evening of the week, was like fairyland; a blaze of lanterns and torches lit up the whole city.

In the Court of the Women, in the Temple, all the golden lamps were lit, twinkling and burning like countless stars.

On the steps that separated this court from the next one, stood three thousand singers, the sons and daughters of the tribe of Levi. Two priests stood at the top of the steps, and as each gave the signal on a great silver trumpet, the burst of song that went up from the vast choir seemed to shake the very heavens. Harps and psalters and flutes swelled with the rolling waves of the organ's melody. To the sound of this music, men marched with flaming torches in their hands, and the marching and a weird torch-dance were kept up until the gates of the Temple closed.

In the midst of all the feasting and the gayeties that followed, the long-expected Voice was heard in the arcades of the Temple.

The Child of Nazareth was once more in His Father's house about His Father's business.

On the last great day of the feast, Joel was up at day-break, ready to follow the older members of the family as soon as the first trumpet-blast should sound.

In his right hand he carried a citron, as did all the others; in his left was a palm-branch, the emblem of joy. An immense multitude gathered at the spring of Siloam. Water was drawn in a golden pitcher, and carried back to be poured on the great altar, while the choir sang with its thousands of voices, and all the people shouted, Amen and Amen!

When the days had gone by in which the seventy bullocks had been sacrificed, and when the ceremonies were all over, then the leaves were stripped from the green booths, and the people scattered to their homes.

Long afterward, Jesse remembered only the torch-light dances, the silver trumpets and the crowds, and the faint ringing of the fringe of bells on the priest's robes as he carried the fire on the golden shovel to burn the sweet-smelling incense.

Joel's memory rang often with two cries that had startled the people. One when the water was poured from the golden pitcher. It was the Master's voice: "*If any man thirst, let him come unto me.*" The other was when all eyes were turned on the blazing lamps. "*I am the Light of the World!*"

Reuben thought oftenest of the blind man to whom he had seen sight restored. But Lazarus was filled with anxiety and foreboding; through his office of scribe, he had come in close contact with the men who were plotting against his friend. Dark rumors were afloat. The air was hot with whisperings of hate.

He had overheard a conversation between the Temple police, and some of the chief priests and Pharisees.

"Why did ye not take Him, as ye were ordered?" they demanded angrily.

"We could not," was the response; "for never man spake like this man."

He had seen the mob searching for stones to throw at Him. Though He had disappeared out of their midst unhurt, still Lazarus felt that some terrible disaster was hanging threateningly over the head of his beloved friend.

CHAPTER XII.

T was with a deep feeling of relief that the two families watched the Master go away into Perea. Phineas still kept with Him. As the little band disappeared down the street, Ruth hid her face in her mother's dress and began to cry.

"I don't want my father to go away again!" she sobbed. Abigail took her in her lap and tried to comfort her, although there were tears in her own eyes.

"We will go home soon, little daughter, and then father will be with us all the time. But we must wait first, till after the cold, rainy season, and the Feast of Dedication."

"What! another feast?" asked Jesse, to whom the summer had seemed one long confusion of festivals. "Don't they have lots of them down in this country! What's this one for?"

"Grandfather will tell you," answered his mother. "Run out and ask him for the story. I know you will like it."

Seated on his grandfather's knee, Jesse doubled up his little fists, as he heard how a heathen altar had once been set up on the great altar of burnt-offering, and a heathen general had driven a herd of swine through the holy Temple, making it unclean. But his breath came quick, and his eyes shone, as the proud old Israelite told him of Judas the Maccabee, Judas the lion-hearted, who had whipped the Syrian soldiers, purified the Temple, and dedicated it anew to the worship of Jehovah.

"Our people never forget their heroes," ended the old man. "Every year, in every home, no matter how humble, one candle is lighted at the beginning of the feast; the next night, two, and the next night, three, and so on, till eight candles shine out into the winter darkness.

"For so the brave deeds of the Maccabees burn in the memory of every child of Abraham!"

The feast came and went. While the candles burned in every home, and the golden lamps in the great Temple blazed a welcome, the Nazarene came back to His Father's house, to be once more about His Father's business.

Joel caught a glimpse of Him walking up and down the covered porches in front of the Gate Beautiful. The next moment he was pushing

JOEL: A BOY OF GALILEE. 161

and elbowing his way through the jostling crowds, till he stood close beside Him.

After that, the services that followed were a blank. He saw only one face,— the face that had looked into his beside the Galilee, and drawn from his heart its intensest love. He heard only one voice, — the voice he had longed for all these weeks and days. Just to be near Him! To be able to reach out reverent fingers and only touch the clothes He wore; to look up in His face, and look and look with a love that never wearied, — that was such happiness that Joel was lost to everything else!

But after a while he began to realize that it was for no friendly purpose that the chief priests came pressing around with questions.

"If Thou be the Christ, tell us plainly," they demanded. Then up and down through the long Porch of Solomon, among all its white marble pillars, they repeated His answer: —

"The works that I do in my Father's name, they bear witness of me. I and my Father are one!"

"Blasphemy!" shouted a mocking voice behind Him. "Blasphemy!" echoed Pharisee and Sadducee for once agreed. The crowds pushed and shoved between the pillars; some ran out for stones. In the confusion of the uproar, as they turned to lay violent hands on Him, He slipped out of their midst, and went quietly away.

Joel hunted around awhile for the party he had come with, but seeing neither Phineas nor Lazarus, started back to Bethany on the run. A cold winter rain had begun to fall.

None of Reuben's family had gone into Jerusalem that day on account of the weather, but were keeping the feast at home.

They were startled when the usually quiet boy burst excitedly into the house, and told them what he had just seen.

"O mother Abigail!" he cried, throwing himself on his knees beside her. "If He goes away again may I not go with Him? I *cannot* go back to Galilee and leave Him, unknowing what is to happen. If He is to be persecuted and driven out, and maybe killed, let me at least share His suffering, and be with Him at the last!"

"You forget that He has all power, and that His enemies can do Him no harm," said Abigail, gently. "Has He not twice walked out unharmed, before their very eyes, when they would have taken Him? And besides what good could you do, my boy? You forget you are only a child, and might not be able to stand the hardships of such a journey."

"I am almost fourteen," said Joel, stretching himself up proudly. "And I am as strong now as some of the men who go with Him. *He* gave me back my strength, you know. Oh, you do not know how I love Him!" he cried. "When I am away from Him, I feel as you would were you separated from Jesse and Ruth and father Phineas. My heart is always going out after Him!"

"Child, have you no care for us?" she responded reproachfully.

"Oh, do not speak so!" he cried, catching up her hand and kissing it. "I *do* love you; I can never be grateful enough for all you have done for me. But, O mother Abigail, you could never understand! You were never lame and felt the power of His healing. You were never burning with a wicked hatred, and felt the balm of His forgiveness! You cannot understand how He draws me to Him!"

"Let the boy have his way," spoke up Reuben. "I, too, have felt that wonderful power that draws all men to Him. Gladly would I part with every shekel I possess, if I thereby might win Him the favor of the authorities."

When once more a little band of fugitives followed their Master across the Jordan, Joel was with them.

The winter wore away, and they still tarried Day by day, they were listening to the simple words that dropped like seeds into their memories, to spring up in after months and bear great truths. Now they heard them as half understood parables, — the good Samaritan, the barren fig-tree, the prodigal son, the unjust steward.

There was one story that thrilled Joel deeply, — the story of the lost sheep. For he recalled that stormy night in the sheepfold of Nathan ben Obed, and the shepherd who searched till dawn for the straying lamb.

It was only long afterwards that he realized it was the Good Shepherd Himself who told the story, when He was about to lay down His own life for the lost sheep of Israel.

Meanwhile in Bethany, Rabbi Reuben and his wife rejoiced that their daughter's visit stretched out indefinitely.

Jesse openly declared that he intended to stay there always, and learn to be a goldsmith like his grandfather.

Ruth, too, was happy and contented, and

seemed to have forgotten that she ever had any other home. As the early spring days came on, she lived almost entirely out in the sunshine. She had fallen into the habit of standing at the gate to watch for Lazarus every evening when he came back from the Temple. As soon as she saw him turn the corner into their street, she ran to meet him, her fair curls and white dress fluttering in the wind.

No matter how tired he was, or what cares rested heavily on his mind, the pale face always lighted up, and his dark eyes smiled at her coming.

"Lazarus does not seem well, lately," she heard Martha say to her mother one day. "I have been trying to persuade him to rest a few days; but he insists he cannot until he has finished the scroll he is illuminating."

A few days after that he did not go to the city as usual. Ruth peeped into the darkened room where he was resting on a couch; his eyes were closed, and he was so pale it almost frightened her.

He did not hear her when she tiptoed into the room and out again; but the fragrance of the little stemless rose she laid on his pillow aroused him. He opened his eyes and smiled languidly, as he caught sight of her slipping noiselessly through the door.

Her mother, sewing by the window, looked out and saw her running across the street. Jesse was out in front of the house, playing with a ball.

"Who is that boy talking to Jesse?" asked Abigail of Rebecca, who stood in the doorway, holding out her arms as Ruth came up.

"Why, that is little Joseph, the only son of Simon the leper. Poor child!"

"Simon the leper," repeated Abigail. "A stranger to me."

"Surely not. Have you forgotten the wealthy young oil-seller who lived next the synagogue? He has the richest olive groves in this part of the country."

"Not the husband of my little playmate Esther!" cried Abigail. "Surely he has not been stricken with leprosy!"

"Yes; it is one of the saddest cases I ever heard of. It seems so terrible for a man honored as he has been, and accustomed to every luxury, to be such a despised outcast."

"Poor Esther!" sighed Abigail. "Does she ever see him?"

"Not now. The disease is fast destroying

him; and he is such a hideous sight that he has forbidden her to ever try to see him again. Even his voice is changed. Of course he would be stoned if he were to come back. He never seeks the company of other lepers. She has had a room built for him away from the sight of men. Every day a servant carries him food and tidings. It is well that they have money, or he would be obliged to live among the tombs with others as repulsive-looking as himself, and such company must certainly be worse than none. Sometimes little Joseph is taken near enough to speak to him, that he may have the poor comfort of seeing his only child at a distance."

"What if it were my Phineas!" exclaimed Abigail, her tears dropping fast on the needle-work she held. "Oh, it is a thousand times worse than death!"

Out in the street the boys were making each other's acquaintance in the off-hand way boys of that age have.

"My name is Jesse. What's yours?"

"Joseph."

"Where do you live?"

"Around the corner, next to the synagogue."

"My father is a carpenter. What's yours?"

Joseph hesitated. "He used to be an oil-seller," he said finally. "He does n't do anything now."

"Why?" persisted Jesse.

"He is a leper now," was the reluctant answer.

A look of distress came over Jesse's face. He had seen some lepers once, and the sight was still fresh in his mind. As they were riding down from Galilee, Joel had pointed them out to him. A group of beggars with horrible scaly sores that had eaten away their flesh, till some were left without lips or eyelids; one held out a deathly white hand from which nearly all the fingers had dropped. Their hair looked like white wire, and they called out, in shrill, cracked voices, "Unclean! Unclean! Come not near us!"

"How terrible to have one's father like that," thought Jesse. A lump seemed to come up in his throat; his eyes filled with tears at the bare idea. Then, boy-like, he tossed up his ball, and forgot all about it in the game that followed.

Several days after he met Joseph and a servant who was carrying a large, covered basket and a water-bottle made of skin.

"I'm going to see my father, now," said Joseph. "Ask your mother if you can come with me."

Jesse started towards his home, then turned suddenly. "No, I'm not going to ask her, for she'll be sure to say no. I am just going anyhow."

"You'll catch it when you get home!" exclaimed Joseph.

"Well, it cannot last long," reasoned Jesse, whose curiosity had gotten the better of him. "I believe I'd rather take a whipping than not to go."

Joseph looked at him in utter astonishment.

"Yes, I would," he insisted; "so come on!"

A short walk down an unfrequented road, in the direction of Jericho, took them to a lonely place among the bare cliffs. A little cabin stood close against the rocks, with a great sycamore-tree bending over it. Near by was the entrance to a deep cave, always as cool as a cellar, even in the hottest summer days.

At the mouth of the cave sat Simon the leper. He stood up when he saw them coming, and wrapped himself closely in a white linen mantle that covered him from head to foot. It was a ghostly sight to Jesse; but to Joseph, so long accustomed to it, there seemed nothing strange.

At a safe distance the servant emptied his basket on a large flat rock, and poured the water into a stone jar standing near. Last of all, he laid a piece of parchment on the stone. It was Esther's daily letter to her exiled husband.

No matter what storms swept the valley, or what duties pressed at home, that little missive was always sent. She had learned to write for his sake. By all his friends he was accounted dead; but her love, stronger than death, bridged the gulf that separated them. She lived only to minister to his comfort as best she could.

Simon did not send as long a message in return as this trusted messenger usually carried. He had much to say to his boy, and the sun was already high.

Jesse, lagging behind in the shelter of the rock, heard the tender words of counsel and blessing that came from the white-sheeted figure with a feeling of awe.

As the father urged his boy to be faithful to every little duty, careful in learning the prayers, and above all obedient to his mother, Jesse's conscience began to prick him sorely.

"I believe I know somebody that could cure him," he said, as they picked their way over the rocks, going home. "'Cause He made Joel well."

"Who's Joel?" asked Joseph.

"A boy that lives with us. He was just as lame, and limped way over when he walked. Now he is as straight as I am. All the sick people where I lived went to Him, and they got well."

Joseph shook his head. "Lepers can't be cured. Can they, Seth?" he asked, appealing to the servant.

"No, lepers are just the same as dead," answered Seth. "There's no help for them."

Jesse was in a very uncomfortable frame of mind, as, hot and dusty, he left his companion and dragged home at a snail's pace.

Next morning Joseph was waiting for him out in front. "Well, did she whip you?" he asked, with embarrassing frankness.

"No," said Jesse, a little sheepishly. "She put me to bed just as soon as I had eaten my dinner, and made me stay there till this morning."

CHAPTER XIII.

UTH went every day to ask for her sick friend, sometimes with a bunch of grapes, sometimes with only a flower in her warm little hand.

But there came a time when Martha met her, with eyes all swollen and red from crying, and told her they had sent to the city for a skilful physician.

In the night there came a loud knocking at the door, and a call for Rabbi Reuben to come quickly, that Lazarus was worse. At day-break a messenger was sent clattering away to hurry over the Jordan in hot haste, and bring back from Perea the only One who could help them.

The noise awakened Ruth; she sat up in surprise to see her mother dressed so early. The outer door was ajar, and she heard the message that the anxious Martha bade the man deliver: "Lord, he whom Thou lovest is sick."

"He will come right away and make him well, won't He, mother?" she asked anxiously.

"Surely, my child," answered Abigail. "He loves him too well to let him suffer so."

But the day wore on, and the next; still another, and He did not come.

Ruth stole around like a frightened shadow, because of the anxious looks on every face.

"Why does n't He come?" she wondered; and on many another lip was the same question.

She was so quiet, no one noticed when she stole into the room where her friend lay dying. Mary knelt on one side of the bed, Martha on the other, watching the breath come slower and slower, and clinging to the unresponsive hands as if their love could draw him back to life.

Neither shed a tear, but seemed to watch with their souls in their eyes, for one more word, one more look of recognition.

Abigail sat by the window, weeping softly. Ruth had never seen her mother cry before, and it frightened her. She glanced at her grandfather, standing by the foot of the bed; two great tears rolled slowly down his cheeks, and dropped on his long beard.

A sudden cry from Mary, as she fell fainting

to the floor, called her attention to the bed again. Martha was silently rocking herself to and fro, in an agony of grief.

Still the child did not understand. Those in the room were so busy trying to bring Mary back to consciousness, that no one noticed Ruth.

Drawn by some impulse she could not understand, the child drew nearer and nearer. Then she laid her soft little hand on his, thinking the touch would surely make him open his eyes and smile at her again; it had often done so before.

But what was it that made her start back terrified, and shrink away trembling? It was not Lazarus she had touched, but the awful mystery of death.

"I did not know that a little child could feel so deeply," said Abigail to her mother, when she found that Ruth neither ate nor played, but wandered aimlessly around.

"I shall keep her away from the funeral."

But all her care could not keep from the little one's ears the mournful music of the funeral dirge, or the wailing of the mourners, who gathered to do honor to the young man whom all Bethany knew and loved.

Many friends came out from Jerusalem to

follow the long procession to the tomb. There was a long eulogy at the grave; but the most impressive ceremony was over at last, and the great stone had to be rolled into the opening that formed the doorway.

Then the two desolate sisters went back to their lonely home and empty life, wondering how they could go on without the presence that had been such a daily benediction.

The fourth day after his death, as Martha sat listlessly looking out of the green arbor with unseeing eyes, Ruth ran in with a radiant face.

"He's come!" she cried. "He's come, and so has my father. Hurry! He is waiting for you!"

Martha drew her veil about her, and mechanically followed the eager child to the gate, where Phineas met her with the same message.

"Oh, why did He not come sooner?" she thought bitterly, as she pressed on after her guide.

Once outside of the village, she drew aside her veil. There stood the Master, with such a look of untold sympathy on His worn face, that Martha cried out, "Lord, if Thou hadst been here my brother had not died!"

"Thy brother shall rise again," He said gently.

"Yes, I know he shall rise again in the resurrection, at the last day," she said brokenly. "That brings hope for the future; but what comfort is there for the lonely years we must live without him?" The tears streamed down her face again.

Then for the first time came those words that have brought balm into thousands of broken hearts, and hope into countless tear-blind eyes.

"I am the resurrection and the life. He that believeth in me shall never die. Believest thou this?"

Martha looked up reverently. "Yea, Lord, I believe that Thou art the Christ, the Son of God which should come into the world."

A great peace came over her troubled spirit as she hurried to her home, where the many friends still sat who had come to comfort them. A number of them were from Jerusalem, and she knew that among them were some who were unfriendly to her brother's friend.

So she quietly called her sister from the room, whispering, "The Master is come, and calleth for thee!"

Those who sat there thought they were going to the grave to weep, as was the custom. So they rose also, and followed at a little distance.

Mary met Him with the same exclamation that her sister had uttered, and fell at His feet.

He, seeing in her white face the marks of the deep grief she had suffered, was thrilled to the depths of His humanity by the keenest sympathy. His tears fell too, at the sight of hers.

"Behold how He loved Lazarus!" said a man to the one who stood beside him.

"Why did He not save him then?" was the mocking answer.

"They say He has the power to open the eyes of the blind, and even to raise the dead. Let Him show it in this case!"

It was a curious crowd that followed Him to the door of the tomb: men who hated Him for the scorching fire-brands of rebuke He had thrown into their corrupt lives; men who feared Him as a dangerous teacher of false doctrines; men who knew His good works, but hesitated either to accept or refuse; and men who loved Him better than life,— all waiting, wondering what He would do.

"Roll the stone away!" He commanded; a dozen strong shoulders bent to do His bidding. Then He looked up and spoke in a low tone, but so distinctly that no one lost a word.

"Father," He said,— He seemed to be speaking

to some one just beside Him, — "I thank Thee that Thou hast heard me, and I knew that Thou hearest me always: but because of the people which stand by I said it, that they may believe that Thou hast sent me."

A cold shiver of expectancy ran over those who heard. Then He cried, in a loud voice, "*Lazarus, come forth!*" There was a dreadful pause. Some of the women clutched each other with frightened shrieks; even strong men fell back, as out of the dark grave walked a tall figure wrapped in white grave-clothes.

His face was hidden in a napkin. "Loose him, and let him go," said the Master, calmly.

Phineas stepped forward and loosened the outer bands. When the napkin fell from his face, they saw he was deathly white; but in an instant a warm, healthful glow took the place of the corpse-like pallor.

Not till he spoke, however, could the frightened people believe that it was Lazarus, and not a ghost they saw.

Never had there been such a sight since the world began: the man who had lain four days in the tomb, walking side by side with the man who had called him back to life.

The streets were full of people, laughing,

shouting, crying, fairly beside themselves with astonishment.

Smiths left their irons to cool on the anvils; bakers left their bread to burn in the ovens; the girl at the fountain dropped her half-filled pitcher; and a woman making cakes ran into the street with the dough in her hands.

Every house in the village stood empty, save one where a sick man moaned for water all unheeded, and another where a baby wakened in its cradle and began to cry.

Long after the reunited family had gone into their home with their nearest friends, and shut the door on their overwhelming joy, the crowds still stood outside, talking among themselves.

Many who had taken part against the Master before, now believed on account of what they had seen. But some still said, more openly than before, " He is in league with the evil one, or He could not do such things." These hurried back to Jerusalem, to spread the report that this dangerous man had again appeared, almost at the very gates of the great Capital.

That night there was a secret council of the chief priests and the Pharisees. " What shall we do," was the anxious question. " If we let Him alone, all men will believe on Him; and the Romans shall come and take away both our place and our nation."

Every heart beat with the same thought, but only Caiaphas put it in words. At last he dared repeat what he had only muttered to himself before: "It is expedient for us that one man should die for the people, and that the whole nation perish not."

While the streets were still full of people, Jesse crept up to Joel, as they sat together in the court-yard. "Don't you think it would be just as easy to cure a leper as to raise Rabbi Lazarus from the dead?"

"Yes, indeed!" answered Joel, positively, "I've seen it done."

"Oh, have you?" cried the boy, in delight. "Then Joseph can have his father back again."

He told him the story of Simon the leper, and of his visit to the lonely cave.

Joel's sympathies were aroused at once. Ever since his own cure, he had felt that he must bring every afflicted one in the wide world to the great source of healing.

Just then a man stopped at the gate to ask for Phineas. Joel had learned to know him well, in the weeks they had been travelling together; it was Thomas.

The boy sprang up eagerly. "Do you know when the Master is going to leave Bethany?" he asked.

"In the morning," answered Thomas, "and right glad I am that it is to be so soon. For when we came down here, I thought it was but to die with Him. He is beset on all sides by secret enemies."

"And will He go out by the same road that we came?"

"It is most probable."

Joel waited for no more information from him, but went back to Jesse to learn the way to the cave.

Jesse was a little fellow, but a keen-eyed one, and was able to give Joel the few simple directions that would lead him the right way.

"Oh, I'm so glad you are going!" he exclaimed. "Shall I run and tell Joseph what you are going to do?"

"No, do not say a word to any one," answered Joel. "I shall be back in a very short time."

CHAPTER XIV.

SIMON the leper sat at the door of his cave. He held a roll of vellum in his unsightly fingers; it was a copy of the Psalms that Lazarus had once made for him in happier days.

Many a time he had found comfort in these hope-inspiring songs of David; but to-day he was reading a wail that seemed to come from the depths of his own soul:

"Thy wrath lieth hard upon me, and Thou hast afflicted me with all Thy waves. Thou hast put mine acquaintance far from me. Thou hast made me an abomination unto them. I am shut up and I cannot come forth. Lord, I have called daily upon Thee. I have stretched out my hands unto Thee. Wilt Thou show wonders to the dead? Shall the dead arise again and praise Thee? Lord, why casteth Thou off my soul? Why hidest Thou Thy face from me?"

The roll dropped to the ground, and he hid his face in his hands, crying, "How long must I endure this? Oh, why was I not taken instead of Lazarus?"

The sound of some one scrambling over the rocks made him look up quickly.

Seth never made his visits at this time of the day, and strangers had never before found the path to this out-of-the-way place.

Joel came on, and stopped by the rock where the water-jar stood.

Simon stood up, covering himself with his mantle, and crying out, warningly, "Beware! Unclean! Come no further!"

"I bring you news from the village," said Joel. The man threw out his hand with a gesture of alarm.

"Oh, not of my wife Esther," he cried, imploringly, "or of my little Joseph! I could not bear to hear aught of ill from them. My heart is still sore for the death of my friend Lazarus. I went as near the village as I dared, and heard the dirge of the flutes and the wailing of the women, when they laid him in the tomb. I have sat here ever since in sackcloth and ashes."

"But Lazarus lives again!" exclaimed Joel, simply. He had seen so many miracles lately, that he forgot the startling effect such an announcement would have on one not accustomed to them.

The man stood petrified with astonishment. At last he said bitterly, "You but mock me, boy; at least leave me to my sorrow in peace."

"No!" cried Joel. "As the Lord liveth, I swear it is the truth. Have you not heard that Messiah has come? I have followed Him up and down the country, and know whereof I speak. At a word from Him the dumb sing, the blind see, and the lame walk. I was lame myself, and He made me as you see me now."

Joel drew himself up to his fullest height. Simon looked at him, completely puzzled.

"Why did you take the trouble to come and tell me that, — a poor despised leper?" he finally asked.

"Because I want everybody else to be as happy as I am. He cured me. He gave me back my strength. Then why should not my feet be always swift to bring others to Him for the same happy healing? He Himself goes about all the time doing good. I know there is hope for you, for I have seen Him cleanse lepers."

Simon trembled, as the full meaning of the hope held out to him began to make itself clear

"'YOU BUT MOCK ME, BOY'"

to his confused mind: health, home, Esther, child, — all restored to him. It was joy too great to be possible.

"Oh, if I could only believe it!" he cried.

"Lazarus was raised when he had been four days dead. All Bethany can bear witness to that," persisted Joel. The words poured out with such force and earnestness, as he described the scene, that Simon felt impelled to believe him.

"Where can I find this man?" he asked.

Joel pointed down the rocky slope. "Take that road that leads into Bethany. Come early in the morning, and as we all pass that way, call to Him. He never refuses any who have faith to believe that He can grant what they ask."

When Joel was half-way down the hill, he turned back. "If He should not pass on the morrow," he said, "do not fail to be there on the second day. We will surely leave here soon."

Simon stood in bewilderment till the boy had passed down the hill; he began to fear that this messenger had been only the creation of a dream. He climbed upon the cliff and peered down into the valley. No, he had not been deceived; the boy was no mirage of his thirsty soul, for there, he came out into full sight again, and now, he was climbing the opposite hillside.

"How beautiful upon the mountain are the feet of him who bringeth good tidings!" he murmured. "Oh, what a heaven opens out before me, if this lad's words are only true!"

Next morning, after they left Bethany, Joel looked anxiously behind every rock and tree that they passed; but Simon was not to be seen.

Presently Joel saw him waiting farther down the road; he was kneeling in the dust. The white mantle, that in his sensitiveness was always used to hide himself from view, was cast aside, that the Great Healer might see his great need.

He scanned the approaching figures with imploring eyes. He was looking for the Messiah, — some one in kingly garments, whose jewelled sceptre's lightest touch would lay upon him the royal accolade of health.

These were evidently not the ones he was waiting for. These were only simple wayfarers; most of them looked like Galileans.

He was about to rise up with his old warning cry of unclean, when he caught sight of Joel. But where was the princely Redeemer of prophecy?

Nearer and nearer they came, till he could look full in their faces. No need now to ask on which one he should call for help; indeed, he seemed to see but one face, it was so full of loving pity.

"O Thou Messiah of Israel!" he prayed. "Thou didst call my friend Lazarus from the dead, O pass me not by! Call me from this living death! Make me clean!"

The eyes that looked down into his seemed to search his soul. "Believest thou that I can do this?"

The pleading faith in Simon's eyes could not be refused. "Yea, Lord," he cried, "Thou hast but to speak the word!"

He waited, trembling, for the answer that meant life or death to him.

"I will. Be thou clean!" He put out His hand to raise the kneeling man to his feet. "Go and show thyself to the priests," He added.

The party passed on, and Simon stood looking after them. *Was* it the Christ who had passed by? Where were His dyed garments from Bozrah? The prophet foretold Him as glorious in apparel, travelling in the greatness of His strength. No sceptre of divine power had touched him; it was only the clasp of a warm human hand he had felt. He looked down at himself. Still a leper! His faith wavered; but he remembered he had not obeyed the command to show himself to the priests. Immediately he started across the fields on a run, towards the road leading into Jerusalem.

Far down the highway Joel heard a mighty shout; he turned and looked back. There on the brow of a hill, sharply outlined against the sky, stood Simon. His arms were lifted high up towards heaven; for as he ran, in obedience to the command, the leprosy had gone from him. He was pouring out a flood of praise and thanksgiving, in the first ecstasy of his recovery, at the top of his voice.

Joel thought of the tiresome ceremonies to be observed before the man could go home, and wished that the eight days of purification were over, that the little family might be immediately reunited.

Meanwhile, Seth, with his basket and water-bottle, was climbing the hill toward the cave. For the first time in seven years since he had commenced these daily visits, no expectant voice greeted him. He went quite close up to the little room under the cliff; he could see through the half-open door that it was empty. Then he cautiously approached the mouth of the cave, and called his master. A hundred echoes answered him, but no human voice responded. Call after call was sent ringing into the hollow darkness. The deep stillness weighed heavily upon him; he began to be afraid that somewhere in its mysterious depths lay a dead body.

The fear mastered him. Only stopping to put down the food and pour out the water, he started home at the top of his speed.

As he reached the road, a traveller going to Bethany hailed him. "What think you that I saw just now?" asked the stranger. "A man running with all his might towards Jerusalem. Tears of joy were streaming down his cheeks, and he was shouting as he ran, 'Cleansed! Cleansed! Cleansed!' He stopped me, and bade me say, if I met a man carrying a basket and water-skin, that Simon the leper has just been healed of the leprosy. He will be home as soon as the days of purification are over."

Seth gazed at him stupidly, feeling that he must be in a dream. Esther, too, heard the message unbelievingly. Yet she walked the floor in a fever of excitement, at the bare possibility of such a thing being true.

The next morning, she sent Seth, as usual, with the provisions. But he brought them back, saying the place was still deserted.

Then she began to dare to hope; although she tried to steel herself against disappointment, by whispering over and over that she could never see him again, she waited impatiently for the days to pass. At last they had all dragged by.

The new day would begin at sunset, the very earliest time that she might expect him. The house was swept and garnished as if a king were coming. The table was set with the choicest delicacies Seth could find in the Jerusalem markets.

The earliest roses, his favorite red ones, were put in every room. In her restless excitement nothing in her wardrobe seemed rich enough to wear. She tried on one ornament after another before she was suited. Then, all in white, with jewels blazing in her ears, on her throat, on her little white hands, and her eyes shining like two glad stars, she sat down to wait for him.

But she could not keep still. This rug was turned up at the corner; that rose had dropped its petals on the floor. She would have another kind of wine on the table.

At last she stepped out of the door in her little silken-bound sandals, and climbed the outside stairs to the roof, to watch for him.

The sun was entirely out of sight, but the west

was glorious with the red gold of its afterglow. Looking up the Mount of Olives, she could see the smoke of the evening sacrifice rising as the clouds of incense filled the Temple. Surely he must be far on the way by this time.

Her heart almost stopped beating as she saw a figure coming up the road, between the rows of palm-trees. She strained her eyes for a nearer view, then drew a long tremulous breath. It was Lazarus; there went the two children and the lamb to meet him. All along the street, people were standing in the doors to see him go past; he was still a wonder to them.

She shaded her eyes with her hand, and looked again. But while her gaze searched the distant road, some one was passing just below, under the avenue of leafy trees, with quick impatient tread; some one paused at the vine-covered door; some one was leaping up the stairs three steps at a time; some one was coming towards her with out-stretched arms, crying, "Esther, little Esther, O my wife! My God-given one!"

For the first time in seven years, she turned to find herself in her husband's arms. Strong and well, with the old light in his eyes, the old thrill in his voice, the glow of perfect health tingling through all his veins, he could only whisper tremulously, as he held her close, "Praise God! Praise God!"

No wonder he seemed like a stranger to Joseph. But the clasp of the strong arms, and the deep voice saying "my son," so tenderly, were inexpressibly dear to the little fellow kept so long from his birthright of a father's love.

He was the first to break the happy silence that fell upon them. "What a good man Rabbi Jesus must be, to go about making people glad like this all the time!"

"It is He who shall redeem Israel!" exclaimed Simon. "To God be the glory, who hath sent Him into this sin-cursed world! Henceforth all that I have, and all that I am, shall be dedicated to His service!"

Kneeling there in the dying daylight, with his arms around the wife and child so unexpectedly given back to him, such a heart-felt prayer of gratitude went upward to the good Father that even the happiest angels must have paused to listen, more glad because of this great earth-gladness below.

CHAPTER XV.

"I THINK there will be an unusual gathering of strangers at the Passover this year," said Rabbi Reuben to Lazarus, as they came out together from the city, one afternoon. "The number may even reach three millions. A travelling man from Rome was in my shop to-day. He says that in the remotest parts of the earth, wherever the Hebrew tongue is found, one may hear the name of the Messiah.

"People pacing the decks of the ships, crossing the deserts, or trading in the shops, talk only of Him and His miracles; they have aroused the greatest interest even in Athens and the cities of the Nile. The very air seems full of expectancy. I cannot but think great things are about to come to pass. Surely the time is now ripe for Jesus to proclaim Himself king. I cannot understand why He should hide Himself away in the wilderness as if He feared for His safety."

Lazarus smiled at the old man, with a confident expression. "Be sure, my friend, it is only because the hour has not yet come. What a sight it will be when He does stand before the tomb of our long dead power, to call back the nation to its old-time life and grandeur. I can well believe that with Him all things are possible."

"Would that this next Passover were the time!" responded Reuben. "How I would rejoice to see His enemies laid low in the dust!"

Already, on the borders of Galilee, the expected king had started toward His coronation. Many of the old friends and neighbors from Capernaum had joined their band, to go on to the Paschal feast.

They made slow progress, however, for at every turn in the road they were stopped by outstretched hands and cries for help. Nearly every step was taken to the sound of some rejoicing cry from some one who had been blessed.

Joel could not crowd all the scenes into his memory; but some stood with clear-cut distinctness. There were the ten lepers who met them at the very outset; and there was blind Bartimeus begging by the wayside. He could never forget the expression of that man's face, when his eyes were opened, and for the first time he looked out on the glory of the morning sunshine.

Joel quivered all over with a thrill of sympathy, remembering his own healing, and realizing more than the others what had been done for the blind beggar.

Then there was Zaccheus, climbing up to look down through the sycamore boughs that he might see the Master passing into Jericho, and Zaccheus scrambling down again in haste to provide entertainment for his honored guest.

There was the young ruler going away sorrowful because the sacrifice asked of him was more than he was willing to make. But there was one scene that his memory held in unfading colors: —

Roses and wild honeysuckle climbing over a bank by the road-side. Orange-trees dropping a heavy fragrance with the falling petals of their white blossoms. In the midst of the shade and the bloom the mothers from the village near by, gathering with their children, all freshly washed and dressed to find favor in the eyes of the passing Prophet.

Babies cooed in their mother's arms. Bright little faces smiled out from behind protecting skirts, to which timid fingers clung. As they waited for the coming procession, and little bare feet chased each other up and down the bank, the happy laughter of the older children filled all the sunny air.

As the travellers came on, the women caught up their children and crowded forward. It was a sight that would have made almost any one pause, — those innocent-eyed little ones waiting for the touch that would keep them always pure in heart, — that blessing their mothers coveted for them.

But some of the disciples, impatient at the many delays, seeing in the rosy faces and dimpled limbs nothing that seemed to claim help or attention, spoke to the women impatiently. "Why trouble ye the Master?" they said. "Would ye stop the great work He has come to do for matters of such little importance?"

Repelled by the rebuke, they fell back. But there was a look of displeasure on His face, such as they had never seen before, as Jesus turned toward them.

"Suffer the little children to come unto me," He said, sternly, "and forbid them not; for of such is the kingdom of heaven!"

Then holding out His hands He took them up in

His arms and blessed them, every one, even the youngest baby, that blinked up at Him unknowingly with its big dark eyes, received its separate blessing.

So fearlessly they came to Him, so lovingly they nestled in His arms, and with such perfect confidence they clung to Him, that He turned again to His disciples. "Verily I say unto you, Whosoever shall not receive the kingdom of God as a little child, he shall not enter therein."

Met at all points as He had been by loathsome sights, ragged beggars, and diseases of all kinds, this group of happy-faced children must have remained long in His memory, as sweet as the unexpected blossoming of a rose in a dreary desert.

At last the slow journey drew towards a close. The Friday afternoon before the Passover found the tired travellers once more in Bethany. News of their coming had been brought several hours before by a man riding down from Jericho. His swift-footed beast had overtaken and passed the slow procession far back on the road.

There was a joyful welcome for the Master in the home of Lazarus. The cool, vine-covered arbor was a refreshing change from the dusty road. Here were no curious throngs and constant demands for help.

Away from the sights that oppressed Him, away from the clamor and the criticism, here was a place where heart and body might find rest. The peace of the place, and the atmosphere of sympathy surrounding Him, must have fallen like dew on His thirsty soul. Here, for a few short days, He who had been so long a houseless wanderer was to know the blessedness of a home.

Several hours before the first trumpet blast from the roof of the synagogue proclaimed the approaching Sabbath, Simon hurried to his home.

"Esther," he called in great excitement, "I have seen Him! The Christ! I have knelt at His feet. I have looked in His face. And, oh, only think! — He has promised to sit at our table! To-morrow night, such a feast as has never been known in the place shall be spread before Him. Help me to think of something we may do to show him especial honor."

Esther sprang up at the news. "We have very little time to prepare," she said. "Seth must go at once into the city to make purchases. To-morrow night, no hireling hand shall serve him. I myself shall take that lowly place, with Martha and Mary to aid me. Abigail, too, shall help us, for it is a labor of love that she will delight to take part in. I shall go at once to ask them."

The long, still Sabbath went by. The worshippers in the synagogue looked in vain for other miracles, listened in vain for the Voice that wrought such wonders.

Through the unbroken rest of that day He was gathering up His strength for a coming trial. Something of the approaching shadow may have been seen in His tender eyes; some word of the awaiting doom may have been spoken to the brother and sisters sitting reverently at his feet, — for they seemed to feel that a parting was at hand, and that they must crowd the flying hours with all the loving service they could render Him.

That night at the feast, as Esther's little white hands brought the water for the reclining guests to wash, and Martha and Abigail placed sumptuously filled dishes before them, Mary paused in her busy passing to and fro; she longed to do some especial thing to show her love for the honored guest.

Never had His face worn such a look of royalty; never had He seemed so much the Christ. The soft light of many candles falling on His worn face seemed to reveal as never before the divine soul soon to leave the worn body where it now tarried.

An old Jewish custom suddenly occurred to her. She seemed to see two pictures: one was Aaron, standing up in the rich garments of the priesthood, with his head bowed to receive the sacred anointing; the other was Israel's first king, on whom the hoary Samuel was bestowing the anointing that proclaimed his royalty. Token of both priesthood and kingship, — oh, if she dared but offer it!

No one noticed when she stepped out after awhile, and hurried swiftly homeward. Hidden away in a chest in her room, was a little alabaster flask, carefully sealed. It held a rare sweet perfume, worth almost its weight in gold.

She took it out with trembling fingers, and hid it in the folds of her long flowing white dress. Her breath came quick, and her heart beat fast, as she slipped in behind the guests again. The color glowed and paled in her cheeks, as she stood there in the shadow of the curtains, hesitating, half afraid to venture.

At last, when the banquet was almost over, she stepped noiselessly forward. There was a hush of surprise at this unusual interruption, although every one there was familiar with the custom, and recognized its deep meaning and symbolism.

First on His head, then on His feet, she poured the costly perfume. Bending low in the deepest humility, she swept her long soft hair across them to wipe away the crystal drops. The whole house was filled with the sweet, delicate odor.

Some of those who saw it, remembered a similar scene in the house of another Simon, in far away Galilee; but only the Anointed One could feel the deep contrast between the two.

That Simon, the proud Pharisee, condescending and critical and scant in hospitality; this Simon, the cleansed leper, ready to lay down his life, in his boundless love and gratitude. That woman, a penitent sinner, kneeling with tears before His mercy; this woman, so pure in heart that she could see God though hidden in the human body of the Nazarene. That anointing, to His priesthood at the beginning of His ministry; this anointing, to His kingdom, now almost at hand. No one spoke as the fragrance rose and spread itself like the incense of a benediction. It seemed a fitting close to this hour of communion with the Master.

Across this eloquent silence that the softest

sound would have jarred upon, a cold, unfeeling voice broke harshly.

It was Judas Iscariot who spoke. "Why was all this ointment wasted?" he asked. "It would have been better to have sold it and given it to the poor."

Simon frowned indignantly at this low-browed guest, who was so lacking in courtesy, and Mary looked up distressed.

"Let her alone!" said the Master, gently. "Ye have the poor with you always, and whensoever ye will, ye may do them good: but me ye have not always. She hath done what she could: she is come aforehand to anoint my body to the burying."

A dark look gleamed in the eyes of Judas, — there was that reference again to His burial. There seemed to be no use of making any further pretence to follow Him any longer. His kingdom was a delusion, — a vague, shadowy, spiritual thing that the others might believe in if they chose. But if there was no longer any hope of gaining by His service, he would turn to the other side.

That night there was another secret council of some of the Sanhedrin, and Judas Iscariot was in their midst.

"A DARK FIGURE WENT SKULKING OUT INTO THE NIGHT"

When the lights were out, and the Temple police were making their final rounds, a dark figure went skulking out into the night, and wound its way through the narrow streets, — the dark figure that still goes skulking through the night of history, — the man who covenanted for thirty pieces of silver to betray his Lord.

CHAPTER XVI.

"WHO is that talking in the house?" asked Joel of Abigail the morning after the feast. He had been playing in the garden with Jesse, and paused just outside the door as he heard voices.

"Only father and Phineas, now," answered Abigail. "Simon the oil-seller has just been here, and I am sure you could not guess his errand. It was about you."

"About me?" echoed Joel, in surprise.

"Yes, I never knew until this morning that you were the one who persuaded him to go to the Master for healing. He says if it had not been for you, he would still be an outcast from home. During these weeks you have been away, he has been hoping to find some trace of you, for he longs to express his gratitude. Last night at the feast, he learned your name, and now he has just been here to talk to Phineas and father about you. His olive groves yield him a large fortune every year, and he is in a position to do a great deal for you, if you will only let him."

"What does he want to do?" asked Joel.

"He has offered a great deal: to send you to the best schools in the country; to let you travel in foreign lands, and see life as it is in Rome and Athens and the cities of Egypt. Then when you are grown, he offers to take you in business with himself, and give you the portion of a son. It is a rare chance for you, my boy."

"Yes," answered Joel, flushing with pleasure at the thought of all he might be able to see and learn. He seemed lost for a few minutes in the bright anticipation of such a tempting future; then his face clouded.

"But I would have to leave everybody I love," he cried, "and the home where I have been so happy! I cannot do it, mother Abigail; it is too much to ask."

"Now you talk like a child," she answered, half impatiently; but there was a suspicion of tears in her eyes as she added, "Joel, you have grown very dear to us. It will be hard to give you up, for you seem almost like an own son. But consider, my boy; it would not be right to turn away from such advantages. Jesse and Ruth will be well provided for. All that my father has will be theirs some day. But Phineas is only a poor carpenter, and cannot give you much beyond food and clothing. I heard him say just now that he clearly thought it to be your duty to accept, and he had no doubt but that you would."

"But I cannot be with the Master!" cried Joel, as the thought suddenly occurred to him that he could no longer follow Him as he had been doing, if he was to be sent away to study and travel.

"No; but think what you may be able to do for His cause, if you have money and education and influence. It seems to me that for His sake alone, you ought to consent to such an arrangement."

That was the argument that Phineas used when he came out; and the boy was sadly bewildered between the desire to be constantly with his beloved Master, and his wish to serve Him as they suggested.

It was in this perplexed state of mind that he started up to Jerusalem with Jesse and his grandfather.

The streets were rapidly filling with people,

coming up to the Feast of the Passover, and Joel recognized many old friends from Galilee.

"There is Rabbi Amos!" he exclaimed, as he caught sight of an old man in the door of a house across the street. "May I run and speak to him?"

"Certainly!" answered Reuben. "You know your way so well about the streets that it makes no difference if we do get separated. Jesse and I will walk on down to the shop. You can meet us there."

Rabbi Amos gave Joel a cordial greeting. "I am about to go back to the Damascus gate," he said. "I have just been told that the Nazarene will soon make His entrance into the city, and a procession of pilgrims are going out to meet Him. I have heard much of the man since He left Capernaum, and I have a desire to see Him again. Will you come?"

The old man hobbled along so painfully, leaning on his staff, that they were a long time in reaching the gate. The outgoing procession had already met the coming pilgrims, and were starting to return. The way was strewn with palm branches and the clothes they had taken off to lay along the road in front of the man they wished to honor. Every hand carried a palm branch, and every voice cried a Hosannah.

At first Joel saw only a confused waving of the green branches, and heard an indistinct murmur of voices; but as they came nearer, he caught the words, " Hosannah to the Son of David!"

" Look!" cried Rabbi Amos, laying his wrinkled, shaking hand heavily on Joel's shoulder. " Look ye, boy, the voice of prophecy! No Roman war-horse bears the coming victor! It is as Zechariah foretold! That the king should come riding upon the colt of an ass, — the symbol of peace. So David rode, and so the Judges of Israel came and went!"

Joel's eyes followed the gesture of the tremulous, pointing finger. There came the Master, right in the face of His enemies, boldly riding in to take possession of His kingdom.

At last! No wandering now in lonely wildernesses! No fear of the jealous scribe or Pharisee! The time had fully come. With garments strewn in the way, with palms of victory waving before Him, with psalm and song and the shouting of the multitude, He rode triumphantly into the city.

Joel was roused to the highest pitch of enthusiasm, to see His best beloved friend so honored. People understood Him now; they appreciated Him. The demonstrations of the multitude proved it. He was so happy and excited, he scarcely knew what he was doing. He had no palm branch to wave, but as the head of the procession came abreast with him, and he saw the face of the rider, he was almost beside himself.

He waved his empty hands wildly up and down, cheering at the top of his voice; but his shrillest Hosannahs were heard only by himself. They were only a drop in that mighty surf-beat of sound.

Scarcely knowing what to expect, yet prepared for almost anything, they followed the procession into the city. When they reached the porch of the Temple, the Master had disappeared.

"I wonder where He has gone," said Joel, in a disappointed tone. "I thought they would surely crown Him."

"He evidently did not wish it to be," answered Rabbi Amos. "It would be more fitting that the coronation take place at the great feast. Wait until the day of the Passover."

As they sat in the Court of the Gentiles, resting, Joel told Rabbi Amos of the offer made him by the wealthy oil-dealer Simon.

"Accept it, by all means!" was the old man's advice. "We have seen enough just now to know that a new day is about to dawn for Israel. In Bethany, you will be much nearer the Master than in Capernaum; for surely, after to-day's demonstration, He will take up His residence in the capital. In time you may rise to great influence in the new government soon to be established."

The old rabbi's opinion weighed heavily with Joel, and he determined to accept Simon's offer. Then for awhile he was so full of his new plans and ambitions, he could think of nothing else.

All that busy week he was separated from the Master and His disciples; for it was the first Passover he had ever taken part in. After it was over, he was to break the ties that bound him to the carpenter's family and the simple life in Galilee, and go to live in Simon's luxurious home in Bethany.

So he stayed closely with Phineas and Abigail, taking a great interest in all the great preparations for the feast.

Reuben chose, from the countless pens, a male lamb a year old, without blemish. About two o'clock the blast of two horns announced that the priests and Levites in the Temple were ready, and the gates of the inner courts were opened, that all might bring the lambs for examination.

The priests, in two long rows, caught the blood in great gold and silver vessels, as the animals were killed, and passed it to others behind, till it reached the altar, at the foot of which it was poured out.

Then the lamb was taken up and roasted in an earthen oven, and the feast commenced at sunset on Thursday. The skin of the lamb, and the earthen dishes used, were generally given to the host, when different families lodged together.

As many as twenty were allowed to gather at one table. Reuben had invited Nathan ben Obed, and those who came with him, to partake of his hospitality. Much to Joel's delight, a familiar shock of sunburned hair was poked in at the door, and he recognized Buz's freckled face, round-eyed and open mouthed at this first glimpse of the great city.

During the first hour they were together, Buz kept his squinting eyes continually on Joel. He found it hard to believe that this straight, sinewy boy could be the same pitiful little cripple who had gone with him to the sheepfolds of Nathan ben Obed.

"Say," he drawled, after awhile, "I know where that fellow is who made you lame. I was so upset at seeing you this way that I forgot to tell you. He had a dreadful accident, and you have already had your wish, for he is as blind as that stone."

"Oh, how? Who told you?" cried Joel, eagerly.

"I saw him myself, as we came through Jericho. He had been nearly beaten to death by robbers a few weeks before. It gave him a fever, and both eyes were so inflamed and bruised that he lost his sight."

"Poor Rehum!" exclaimed Joel.

"Poor Rehum!" echoed Buz, in astonishment. "What do you mean by poor Rehum? Aren't you glad? Isn't that just exactly what you planned; or did you want the pleasure of punching them out yourself?"

"No," answered Joel, simply; "I forgave him a year ago, the night before I was healed."

"You forgave him!" gasped Buz, — "you forgave him! A dog of a Samaritan! Why, how could you?"

Buz looked at him with such a wondering, puzzled gaze that Joel did not attempt to explain. Buz might be ignorant of a great many things, but he knew enough to hate the Samaritans, and look down on them with the utmost contempt.

"I don't really believe you could understand it," said Joel, "so it is of no use to try to tell you how or why. But I did forgive him, fully and freely. And if you will tell me just where to find him, I will go after him early in the morning and bring him back with me. The Hand that straightened my back can open his eyes; for I have seen it done many times."

All during the feast, Buz kept stealing searching glances at Joel. He could hardly tell which surprised him most, the straightened body or the forgiving spirit. It was so wonderful to him that he sat speechless.

At the same time, in an upper chamber in another street, the Master and His disciples were keeping the feast together. It was their last supper with Him, although they knew it not. Afterwards they recalled every word and every incident, with loving memory that lingered over each detail; but at the time they could not understand its full import.

The gates were left open on Passover night. While the Master and His followers walked out to the Garden of Gethsemane, where they had often gone together, Joel was questioning Buz as to the exact place where he was to find his old enemy.

"I'll go out very early in the morning," said Joel, as his head touched the pillow. "Very early in the morning, for I want Rehum's eyes to be open just as soon as possible, so that he can see the Master's face. Lord help me to find him to-morrow," he whispered, and with a blessing on his lips for the one he had so long ago forgiven, his eyes closed softly.

Sleep came quickly to him after the fatigue and excitement of the day. In his dreams he saw again the Master's face as He made His triumphal entrance into the city; he heard again the acclamations of the crowd. Then he saw Rabbi Amos and Simon and little Ruth. There was a confused blending of kindly faces; there was a shadow-like shifting of indistinct but pleasant scenes. In the fair dreamland where he wandered, fortune smiled on him, and all his paths were peace.

Sleep on, little disciple, happy in thy dreaming; out in Gethsemane's dark garden steals one to betray thy Lord! By the light of glimmering lanterns and fitful torches they take Him now. Armed with swords and staves, they lead Him out from the leafy darkness into the moon-flooded highroad.

Now He stands before the High Priest, — alone, unfriended. Sleep, and wake not at the cock's shrill crowing, for there is none to make answer for Him, and one who loved Him hath thrice denied!

Dream on! In the hall of Pilate now, thorn-crowned and purple-clad, Him whom thou lovest; scourged now, and spat upon. This day, indeed, shall He come into His kingdom, but well for thee, that thou seest not the coronation.

Sleep on, little disciple, be happy whilst thou can!

CHAPTER XVII.

T was so much later than he had intended, when Joel awoke next morning, that without stopping for anything to eat, he hurried out of the city, and took the road by which the Master had made such a triumphal entry a few days before.

Faded branches of palms still lay scattered by the wayside, thickly covered with dust.

All unconscious of what had happened the night before, and what was even at that very moment taking place, Joel trudged on to Bethany at a rapid pace, light-hearted and happy.

For six days he had been among enthusiastic Galileans who firmly believed that before the end of Passover week they should see the overthrow of Rome, and all nations lying at the feet of a Jewish king. How long they had dreamed of this hour!

He turned to look back at the city. The white and gold of the Temple dazzled his eyes, as it threw back the rays of the morning sun. He thought of himself as he had stood that day on the roof of the carpenter's house, stretching out longing arms to this holy place, and calling down curses on the head of his enemy, Rehum.

Could he be the same boy? It seemed to him now that that poor, crippled body, that bitter hatred, that burning thirst for revenge, must have belonged to some one else, he felt so well, so strong, so full of love to God and all mankind.

A little broken-winged sparrow fluttered feebly under a hedgerow. He stopped to gather a handful of ripe berries for it, and even retraced his steps to a tiny spring he had noticed farther back, to bring it water in the hollow of a smooth stone.

He did not find Rehum at the place where Buz had told him to inquire. His father had taken him to his home, somewhere in Samaria.

Joel turned back, tired and disappointed. He was glad to lie down, when he reached Bethany again, and rest awhile. A peculiar darkness began to settle down over the earth. Joel was perplexed and frightened; he knew it could not be an eclipse, for it was the time of the full moon. Finally he started back to Jerusalem, although it was like travelling in the night, for the darkness had deepened and deepened for nearly three hours, and the mysterious gloom made him long to be with his friends.

His first thought was to find the Master, and he naturally turned toward the Temple. Just as he started across the Porch of Solomon, the darkness was lifted, and everything seemed to dance before his eyes. He had never experienced an earthquake shock before, but he felt sure that this was one.

He braced himself against one of the pillars. How the massive columns quivered! How the hot air throbbed! The darkness had been awful, but this was doubly terrifying.

The earth had scarcely stopped trembling, when an old white-bearded priest ran across the Court of the Gentiles; his wrinkled hands, raised above his head, shook as with palsy. The scream that he uttered seemed to transfix Joel with horror.

"*The veil of the Temple is rent in twain!*" he cried, — "*The veil of the Temple is rent in twain!*"

Then with a convulsive shudder he fell forward on his face. Joel's knees shook. The darkness, the earthquake, and now this mighty force that had laid bare the Holy of Holies, filled him with an undefined dread.

He ran past the prostrate priest into the inner

court, and saw for himself. There hung the heavy curtain of Babylonian tapestry, in all its glory of hyacinth and scarlet and purple, torn asunder from top to bottom. No earthquake shock could have made that ragged gash. The wrath of God must have come down and laid mighty fingers upon it.

He ran out of the Temple, and towards the house where he had slept the night before.

The earthquake seemed to have shaken all Jerusalem into the streets. Strange words were afloat. A question overheard in passing one excited group, an exclamation in another, made him run the faster.

At Reuben's shop he found Jesse and Ruth both crying from fright. The attendant who had them in charge told him that his friends had been gone nearly all day.

"Where?" demanded Joel.

"I do not know exactly. They went out with one of the greatest multitudes that ever passed through the gates of the city. Not only Jews, but Greeks and Romans and Egyptians. You should have seen the camels and the chariots, the chairs and the litters!" exclaimed the man.

A sudden fear fell upon the boy that this was the day that the One he loved best had been made king, and he had missed it, — had missed the greatest opportunity of his life.

"Was it to follow Rabbi Jesus of Nazareth?" he demanded eagerly.

The man nodded.

"To crown Him?" was the next breathless question.

"No; to crucify Him."

The unexpected answer was almost a death-thrust. Joel stood a moment, dumb with horror. The blood seemed to stand still in his veins; there was a roaring in his ears; then everything grew black before him. He clutched blindly at the air, then staggered back against the wall.

"No, *no, no,* NO!" he cried; each word was louder than the last. "I will not believe it! You do not speak truth!"

He ran madly from the shop, down the street, and through the city gate. Out on the highway he met the returning multitude, most of them in as great haste as he.

Everything he saw seemed to confirm the truth of what he had just heard, but he could not believe it.

"No, no, no!" he gasped, in a breathless whisper, as he ran. "No, no, no! It cannot be! He is the Christ! The Son of God! They could not be able to do it, no matter how much they hated Him!"

But even as he ran he saw the hill where three crosses rose. He turned sick and cold, and so weak he could scarcely stand. Still he stumbled resolutely on, but with his face turned away from the sight he dared not look upon, lest seeing should be knowing what he feared.

At last he reached the place, and, shrinking back as if from an expected blow, he slowly raised his eyes till they rested on the face of the dead body hanging there.

The agonized shriek on his lips died half uttered, as he fell unconscious at the foot of the cross.

A long time after, one of the soldiers happening to notice him, turned him over with his foot, and prodded him sharply with his spear. It partially aroused him, and in a few moments he sat up. Then he looked up again into the white face above him; but this time the bowed head awed him into a deep calm.

The veil of the Temple was rent indeed, and through this pierced body there shone out from its Holy of Holies the Shekinah of God's love for a dying world. It uplifted Joel, and drew him, and drew him, till he seemed to catch a faint glimpse of the Father's face; to feel himself folded in boundless pardon, in pity so deep, and a love so unfathomed, that the lowest sinner could find a share. But while he gazed and gazed into the white face, so glorified in its marble stillness, Joseph of Arimathea stood between him and the cross, giving directions, in a low tone, for the removal of the body.

It seemed to waken Joel out of his trance; and when the bloodstained form was stretched gently on the ground, he forgot his glimpse of heavenly mysteries, he saw no longer the uplifted Christ. He saw instead, the tortured body of the man he loved; the friend for whom he would gladly have given his life.

Almost blinded by the rush of tears, he groped his way on his knees toward it. A mantle of fine white linen had been laid over the lifeless body; but one hand lay stretched out beside Him with a great bloody nail-hole through the palm, — it was the hand that had healed him; the hand that had fed the hungry multitudes; the hand that had been laid in blessing on the heads of little children, waiting by the roadside! With the thought of all it had done for him, with the thought of all it had done for all the countless ones its warm, loving touch had comforted, came the remembrance of the torture it had just suffered.

Joel lay down beside it with a heart-broken moan.

Men came and lifted the body in its spotless covering. Joel did not look up to see who bore it away.

The lifeless hand still hung down uncovered at His side. With his eyes fixed on that, Joel followed, longing to press it to his lips with burning kisses; but he dared not so much as touch it with trembling fingers, — a sense of his unworthiness forbade.

As the silent procession went onward, Joel found himself walking beside Abigail. She had pushed her veil aside that she might better see the still form borne before them; she had stood near by through all those hours of suffering. Her wan face and swollen eyes showed how the force of her sympathy and grief had worn upon her.

Joel glanced around for Phineas. He was one of those who walked before with the motionless burden, his strong brown hands tenderly supporting the Master's pierced feet; his face was as rigid as stone, and seemed to Joel to have grown years older since the night before.

Another swift rush of tears blinded Joel, as he looked at the set, despairing face, and then at what he carried.

O friend of Phineas! O feet that often ran to meet him on the grassy hillsides of Nazareth, that walked beside him at his daily toil, and led him to a nobler living! — Thou hast climbed the mountain of Beatitudes! Thou hast walked the wind-swept waters of the Galilee! But not of this is he thinking now. It is of Thy life's unselfish pilgrimage; of the dust and travel stains of the feet he bears; of the many steps, taken never for self, always for others; of the cure and the comfort they have daily carried; of the great love that hath made their very passing by to be a benediction.

It seemed strange to Joel that, in the midst of such overpowering sorrow, trivial little things could claim his attention. Years afterward he remembered just how the long streaks of yellow sunshine stole under the trees of the garden; he could hear the whirr of grasshoppers, jumping up in the path ahead of them; he could smell the heavy odor of lilies growing beside an old tomb.

The sorrowful little group wound its way to a part of the garden where a new tomb had been hewn out of the rock; here Joseph of Arimathea motioned them to stop. They laid the open bier gently on the ground, and Joel watched them with dry eyes but trembling lips, as they noiselessly prepared the body for its hurried burial.

From time to time as they wound the bands of white linen, powdered with myrrh and aloes, they glanced up nervously at the sinking sun. The Sabbath eve was almost upon them, and the old slavish fear of the Law made them hasten. A low stifled moaning rose from the lips of the women, as the One they had followed so long was lifted up, and borne forever out of their sight, through the low doorway of the tomb.

Strong hands rolled the massive stone in place that barred the narrow opening. Then all was over; there was nothing more that could be done.

The desolate mourners sat down on the grass outside the tomb, to watch and weep and wait over a dead hope and a lost cause.

A deep stillness settled over the garden as they lingered there in the gathering twilight. They grew calm after awhile, and began to talk in low tones of the awful events of the day just dying.

Gradually, Joel learned all that had taken place. As he heard the story of the shame and abuse and torture that had been heaped upon the One he loved better than all the world, his face grew white with horror and indignation.

"Oh, was n't there *one* to stand up for Him?" he cried, with clasped hands and streaming eyes. "Was n't there *one* to speak a word in His defence? O my Beloved!" he moaned. "Out of all the thousands Thou didst heal, out of all the multitudes Thou didst bless, not one to bear witness!"

He rocked himself to and fro on his knees, wringing his hands as if the thought brought him unspeakable anguish.

"Oh, if I had only been there!" he moaned. "If I could only have stood up beside Him and told what He had done for me! O my God! My God! How can I bear it? To think He went to His death without a friend and without a follower, when I loved Him so! All alone! Not one to speak for Him, not one!"

Groping with tear-blinded eyes towards the tomb, the boy stretched his arms lovingly around the great stone that stopped its entrance; then suddenly realizing that he could never go any closer to the One inside, never see Him again, he leaned his head hopelessly against the rock, and gave way to his feeling of utter loneliness and despair.

How long he stood there, he did not know. When he looked up again, the women had gone, and it was nearly dark. Phineas and several other men lingered in the black shadows of the trees, and Joel joined them.

Roman guards came presently. A stout cord was stretched across the stone, its ends firmly fastened, and sealed with the seal of Cæsar. A watch-fire was kindled near by; then the Roman sentinels began their steady tramp! tramp! as they paced back and forth.

High overhead the stars began to set their countless watch-fires in the heavens; then the white full moon of the Passover looked down, and all night long kept its silent vigil over the forsaken tomb of the sleeping Christ.

Abigail had found shelter for the night with friends, in a tent just outside the city; but Joel and Phineas took their way back to Bethany.

Little was said as they trudged along in the moonlight. Joel thought only of one thing, — his great loss, the love of which he had been bereft. But to Phineas this death meant much more than the separation from the best of friends; it meant the death of a cause on which he had staked his all. He must go back to Galilee to be the laughing-stock of his old neighbors. He who they trusted would have saved Israel had been put to death as a felon, — crucified between two thieves! The cause was lost; he was left to face an utter failure.

When the moon went down that morning over the hills of Judea, there were many hearts that mourned the Man of Nazareth, but not a soul in all the universe believed on Him as the Son of God.

Hope lay dead in the tomb of Joseph, with a great stone forever walling it in.

CHAPTER XVIII.

"AKE up, Joel! Wake up! I bring you good tidings, my lad!" It was Abigail's voice ringing cheerily through the court-yard, as she bent over the boy, fast asleep on the hard stones.

All the long Sabbath day after the burial, he had sat listlessly in the shady court-yard, his blank gaze fixed on the opposite wall. No one seemed able to arouse him from his apathy. He turned away from the food they brought him, and refused to enter the house when night came.

Towards morning he had gone over to the fountain for a long draught of its cool water; then overcome by weakness from his continued fast, and exhausted by grief, he fell asleep on the pavement.

Abigail came in and found him there, with the red morning sun beating full in his face. She had to shake him several times before she could make him open his eyes.

He sat up dizzily, and tried to collect his thoughts. Then he remembered, and laid his head wearily down again, with a groan.

"Wake up! Wake up!" she insisted, with such eager gladness in her voice that Joel opened his eyes again, now fully aroused.

"What is it?" he asked indifferently.

"*He is risen!*" she exclaimed joyfully, clasping her hands as she always did when much excited. "I went to His tomb very early in the morning, while it was yet dark, with Mary and Salome and some other women. The stone had been rolled aside; and while we wondered and wept, fearing His enemies had stolen Him away, He stood before us, with His old greeting on His lips, — 'All hail!'"

Joel rubbed his eyes and looked at her. "No, no!" he said wearily, "I am dreaming again!"

He would have thrown himself on the ground as before, his head pillowed on his arm, but she would not let him. She shook his hands with a persistence that could not be refused, talking to him all the while in such a glad eager voice that he slowly began to realize that something had made her very happy.

"What is it, Mother Abigail?" he asked, much puzzled.

"I do not wonder you are bewildered," she cried. "It is such blessed, such wonderful news. Why He is *alive*, Joel, He whom Thou lovest! Try to understand it, my boy! I have just now come from the empty tomb. I saw Him! I spoke with Him! I knelt at His feet and worshipped!"

By this time all the family had come out. Reuben looked at his daughter pityingly, as she repeated her news; then he turned to Phineas.

"Poor thing!" he said, in a low tone. "She has witnessed such terrible scenes lately, and received such a severe shock, that her mind is affected by it. She does not know what she is saying. Did not you yourself help prepare the body for burial, and put it in the tomb?"

"Yes," answered Phineas, "and helped close it with a great stone, which no one man could possibly move by himself. And I saw it sealed with the seal of Cæsar; and when I left it was guarded by Roman sentinels in armor. No man could have opened it."

"But Abigail talks of angels who sat in the empty tomb, and who told them He had risen," replied her father.

Joel, who had overheard this low-toned conversation, got up and stood close beside them.

He had begun to tremble from weakness and excitement.

"Father Phineas," he asked, "do you remember the story we heard from the old shepherd, Heber? The angels told of His birth; maybe she *did* see them in His tomb."

"How can such things be?" queried Reuben, stroking his beard in perplexity.

"That's just what you said when Rabbi Lazarus was brought back to life," piped Jesse's shrill voice, quite unexpectedly, at his grandfather's elbow. He had not lost a word of the conversation. "Why don't you go and see for yourself if the tomb is empty?"

Abigail had gone into the house with her mother, and now the summons to breakfast greeted them. She saw she could not convince them of the truth of her story, so she said no more about it; but her happy face was more eloquent than words.

All day snatches of song kept rising to her lips, — old psalms of thanksgiving, and half whispered hallelujahs. At last Joel and Phineas were both so much affected by her continued cheerfulness, that they began to believe there must be some great cause for it.

Finally, in the waning afternoon, they took

"'THE STONE IS GONE!'"

the road that led from Bethany to the garden where they firmly believed that the Master still lay buried.

As they came in sight of the tomb, Joel clutched Phineas by the arm, and pointed, with a shaking finger, to the dark opening ahead of of them.

"See!" he said, pointing into its yawning darkness. "She was right! The stone is gone!"

It was some time before they could muster up courage to go nearer and look into the sepulchre. When at last they did so, neither spoke a word, but, after one startled look into each other's eyes, turned and left the garden.

It was growing dark as they hurried along the highway homeward. Two men came half running towards the city, in great haste to reach the gates before they should be closed for the night. They were two disciples well known to Phineas.

He stopped them with the question that was uppermost in his mind.

"Yes, He is risen," answered one of the men, breathlessly. "We have seen Him. Hosanna to the Highest! He walked along this road with us as we went to Emmaus."

"Ah, how our hearts burned as He talked

with us by the way!" interrupted the other man.

"Only this hour He sat at meat with us," cried the first speaker. "He broke bread with us, and blessed it as He always used to do. We are running back to the city now to tell the other disciples."

Phineas would have laid a detaining hand on them, but they hurried on, and left him standing in the road, looking wistfully after them.

"It must be true," said Joel, "or they could not have been so nearly wild with joy."

Phineas sadly shook his head. "I wish I could think so," he sighed.

"Let us go home," urged Abigail, the next day, "the Master has bidden His brethren meet Him in Galilee. Let us go. There is hope of seeing Him again in our old home!"

Joel, now nearly convinced of the truth of her belief, was also anxious to go. But Phineas lingered; his plodding mind was slower to grasp such thoughts than the sensitive woman's or the imaginative boy's. One after another he sought out Peter and James and John, and the other disciples who had seen the risen Master, and questioned them closely. Still he tarried for another week.

One morning he met Thomas, whose doubts all along had strengthened his own. He ran against him in the crowded street in Jerusalem. Thomas seized his arm, and, turning, walked beside him a few paces.

"*It is true!*" he said, in a low intense tone, with his lips close to his ear. "I saw Him myself last night; I held His hands in mine! I touched the side the spear had pierced! He called me by name; and I know now beyond all doubt that the Master has risen from the dead, and that He is the Son of God!"

After that, Phineas no longer objected when it was proposed that they should go back to Galilee. The story of the resurrection was too great for him to grasp entirely, still he could not put aside such a weight of evidence that came to him from friends whose word he had always implicitly trusted.

The roads were still full of pilgrims returning from the Passover. As Phineas journeyed on with his little family, he fell in with the sons of Jonah and Zebedee, going back to their nets and their fishing-boats.

The order of procession was constantly shifting, and one morning Joel found himself walking beside John, one of the chosen twelve, who seemed to have understood his Master better than any of the others.

The man seemed wrapped in deep thought, and took no notice of his companion, till Joel timidly touched his sleeve.

"Do *you* believe it is true?" the boy asked.

There was no surprise in the man's face at the abrupt question, he felt, without asking, what Joel meant. A reassuring smile lighted up his face as he laid his hand kindly on Joel's shoulder.

"I know it, my lad; I have been with Him." The quiet positiveness with which he spoke seemed to destroy Joel's last doubt.

"Many things that He said to us come back to me very clearly; and I see now He was trying to prepare us for this."

"Tell me about them," begged Joel, "and about those last hours He was with you. Oh, if I could only have been with Him, too!"

John saw the tears gathering in the boy's eyes, heard the tremble in his voice, and felt a thrill of sympathy as he recognized a kindred love in the little fellow's heart.

So he told Joel of the last supper they had taken together, of the hymn they had sung, and of the watch they had failed to keep, when He took them with Him into the garden of Gethsemane. All the little incidents connected with those last solemn hours, he repeated carefully to the listening boy.

From time to time Joel brushed his hand across his eyes; but a deep calm fell over him as John's voice went on, slowly repeating the words the Master had comforted them with.

"Let not your hearts be troubled: ye believe in God, believe also in me. In my Father's house are many mansions. . . . I go to prepare a place for you. I will come again, and receive you unto myself; that where I am, there ye may be also. . . . If ye loved me, ye would rejoice, because I said, I go unto the Father. . . . These things I have spoken unto you, that in me ye might have peace. In the world ye shall have tribulation: but be of good cheer; I have overcome the world."

Joel made an exclamation as if about to speak, and then stopped. "What is it?" asked John.

"How could He mean that He has overcome the world? Cæsar still rules, and Jerusalem is full of His enemies. I can't forget that they killed Him, even if He has risen."

John stooped to tie his sandal before he answered.

"I have been fitting together different things He told us; and I begin to see how blind we were. Once He called Himself the Good Shepherd who would give his life for his sheep, and said, 'Therefore doth my Father love me, because I lay down my life that I might take it again. No man taketh it from me, but I lay it down of myself. I have power to lay it down, and I have power to take it again.'"

They walked on in silence a few paces, then John asked abruptly, "Do you remember about the children of Israel being so badly bitten by serpents in the wilderness, and how Moses was commanded to set up a brazen serpent in their midst?"

"Yes, indeed!" answered Joel. "All who looked up at it were saved; but those who would not died from the poisonous bites."

"One night," continued John, "a learned man by the name of Nicodemus, one of the rulers, came to the Master with many questions. And I remember one of the answers He gave him. 'As Moses lifted up the serpent in the wilderness, even so must the Son of Man be lifted up, that whosoever believeth in Him should not perish, but have everlasting life.' We did not understand Him then at all. Not till I saw Him lifted up on the cruel cross, did I begin to dimly see what He meant."

A light broke over Joel's face as he remembered the vision he had had that day, kneeling at the foot of the cross; then he stopped still in the road, with his hands clasped in dismay. There suddenly seemed to rise before him the scenes of daily sacrifice in the Temple, when the blood of innocent lambs flowed over the altar; then he thought of the great Day of Atonement, when the poor scape-goat was driven away to its death, laden with the sins of the people.

"Oh, that must be what Isaiah meant!" he cried in distress. "'He was brought as a lamb to the slaughter!' Oh, can it be possible that 'the Lord hath laid on *Him* the iniquity of us all'? What an awful sacrifice!"

The tears streamed down his face as the thought came over him with overwhelming conviction, that it was for *him* that the man he loved so had endured all the horrible suffering of death by crucifixion.

"Why did such a thing have to be?" he asked, looking up appealingly at his companion.

John looked out and up, as if he saw far beyond the narrow, hill-bound horizon, and quoted softly: "*For God so loved the world, that He gave*

His only begotten Son, that whosoever believeth in Him should not perish, but have everlasting life."

Just as the feeling had come to him that morning by the Galilee, and again as he gazed and gazed into the white face on the cross, Joel seemed to feel again the love of the Father, as it took him close into its infinite keeping.

"'Greater love hath no man than this,'" quoted John again, "'that a man lay down his life for his friends.' He is the propitiation for our sins; and not ours only, but also for the sins of the whole world."

It was hard for the child to understand this at first; but this gentle disciple who walked beside him had walked long beside the Master, and in the Master's own way and words taught Joel life's greatest lesson.

CHAPTER XIX.

THEY went back to their simple lives again, — those hardy fishermen, the busy carpenter, and the boy. Phineas was silent and grave. For him, hope still lay dead in that garden tomb near Golgotha; but Joel sang as he worked.

The appointed time was nearing when the Master was to meet them on the mountain. As often as he could, Joel stole away from the moody man at the work-bench, and went down to the beach for more cheerful companionship.

One morning, seeing a fishing-boat that he recognized pulling in quickly to shore, he ran down to see what luck his friends had had during the night.

He held up his hands in astonishment at the great haul of fish the boat held.

"We have been with the Master," explained one of the men. "We toiled all night, and took nothing till we met Him."

Joel listened eagerly while they told him of that meeting in the early dawn, and of the meal they ate together, while the sun came up over the Galilee, and the blue waves whispered their gladness to the beach, as they heard the Master's voice once more.

"Oh, to think that He is in Galilee again!" exclaimed Joel. That thought added purpose and meaning to each new day. Every morning he woke with the feeling, "Maybe I shall see Him before the sun goes down." Every night he went to sleep saying, "He is somewhere near! No telling how soon I may be with Him!"

When the day came on which they were to go to the mountain, Joel was up very early in the morning. He bathed and dressed himself with the care of a priest about to enter the inner courts on some holy errand.

When he started to the mountain, Abigail noticed that he wore his finest headdress of white linen. His tunic was spotless, and, from the corners of his brown and white striped mantle, the blue fringes that the Law prescribed hung smooth as silk.

He did not wait for Phineas or any of his friends. Long before the time, he had climbed the rocky path, and was sitting all alone in the deep shadowed stillness.

The snapping of a twig startled him; the falling of a leaf made him look up hopefully. Any minute the Master might come.

His heart beat so loud it seemed to him that the wood-birds overhead must surely hear it, and be frightened away.

Imagine that scene, you who can, — you who have just seen the earth close over your best-beloved; who have awakened in the lonely night, with that sudden sickening remembrance of loss; who have longed, with a longing like a constant ache, for the voice and the smile and the footstep that have slipped hopelessly beyond recall.

Think of what it would mean, if you knew now, beyond doubt, that all that you had loved and lost would be given back to you before the passing of another hour!

So Joel waited, restless, burning, all in a quiver of expectancy.

Steps began to wind around the base of the mountain. One familiar face after another came in sight, then strange ones, until, by and by, five hundred people had gathered there, and were sitting in reverent, unbroken silence. The soft summer wind barely stirred the leaves; even the twitter of nestlings overhead was hushed.

After awhile, thrilled by some unseen influence,

as a field of grain is swayed by the passing wind, they bowed their heads. The Master stood before them, His hands outspread in blessing.

Joel started forward with a wild desire to throw himself at His feet, and put his arms around them; but a majesty he had never seen before in that gentle face restrained him.

He listened to the voice as it rose and fell with all its old winning tenderness. As you would listen could the dead lips you love move again; as you would greedily snatch up every word, and hide it in your heart of hearts, so Joel listened.

"I go to prepare a place for you. I will come again and receive you unto myself, that where I am there ye may be also. . . . Peace I leave with you. . . . Not as the world giveth, give I unto you. Let not your heart be troubled, neither let it be afraid."

As the beloved voice went on, promising the Comforter that should come when He was gone, all the dread and pain of the coming separation seemed to be lost.

Boy though he was, Joel looked down the years of his life feeling it was only a fleeting shadow, compared with the eternal companionship just promised him.

He would make no moan; he would utter no complaint: but he would take up his life's little day, and bear it after the Master, — a cup of loving service, — into that upper kingdom where there was a place prepared for him.

It was all over so soon. They were left alone on the mountain-side again, with only the sunshine flickering through the leaves, and the wood-birds just beginning to trill to each other once more. But the warm air seemed to still throb with the last words He had spoken: "Lo, I am with you alway, even unto the end of the world."

Phineas came down the mountain with his face all ashine; at last his eyes had been opened.

"He and the Father are one!" he exclaimed to the man walking beside him. "That voice is the same that spake from the midst of the burning bush, and from the summit of Sinai. All these years I have followed the Master, I believed Him to be a perfect man and a great prophet; I believed Him to be 'the rod out of the stem of Jesse' who through Jehovah's hand was to redeem Israel, even as the rod in Aaron's hand smote the floods and made a pathway for our people.

"When I saw Him put to death as a felon, all hope died within me; even to-day I came out here unbelieving. I could not think that I should see Him. How blind we have been all these years! God with us in the flesh, and we did not know Him!"

Joel walked on behind the two, sharing their feeling of exaltation. As they came down into the valley and entered Capernaum, the work-a-day sights and noises seemed to jar on their senses, in this uplifted mood.

A man standing in an open doorway accosted Phineas, and asked when he could commence work on the house he had talked to him about building.

Phineas hesitated, and looked down at the ground, as if studying some difficult problem. In a few minutes he raised his eyes with a look of decision.

"I cannot build it for you at all," he answered.

"Not build it!" echoed the man. "I thought you were anxious for the job."

"So I was," answered the carpenter; "but when I asked for it, I had no belief that the Master could rise from the dead. Just now, on the mountain yonder, I have been with Him. His command is still ringing in my ears: 'Go ye into all the world, and preach the gospel to every creature!'

"Henceforth I give my life to Him, even as He gave His to me. My days are now half spent, but every remaining one shall be used to proclaim, as far and wide as possible, that the risen Christ is the Son of God!"

The man was startled as he looked at Phineas; such a fire of love and purpose seemed to illuminate his earnest face that it was completely transformed.

"Even now," exclaimed Phineas, "will I commence my mission. You are the first one I have met, and I must tell to you this glad new gospel. He died for you! 'God so loved the world, that He gave His only begotten Son, that whosoever believeth in Him should not perish, but have everlasting life!' O my friend, if you could only believe that as I believe it!"

The man shrank back into the doorway, strangely moved by the passionate force of his earnestness.

"I must go up to Jerusalem," continued Phineas, "and wait till power is given us from on high; then I can more clearly see my way. I do not know whether I shall be directed to go into other lands, or to come back here to carry the news to my old neighbors. But it matters not which path is pointed out, the mission has been already given, — to tell the message to every creature my voice can reach."

"And you?" asked the man, pointing to the companion of Phineas.

"I, too, received the command," was the answer, "and I, too, am ready to go to the world's end, if need be!"

"Surely there must be truth in what you say," muttered the man. Then his glance fell on Joel. "You, too?" he questioned.

"Nay, he is but a lad," answered Phineas, before Joel could find words to answer him. "Come! we must hasten home."

Joel talked little during the next few days, and stole away often to think by himself, in the quiet little upper chamber on the roof.

Phineas was making his preparations to go back to Jerusalem; and he urged the boy to go back with him, and accept Simon's offer. Abigail, too, added her persuasions to his; and even old Rabbi Amos came down one day, and sat for an hour under the fig-trees, painting in glowing colors the life that might be his for the choosing.

It was a very alluring prospect; it had been the dream of his life to travel in far countries. He pictured himself surrounded by wealth and culture; he would be able to do so much for his old friends. He could give back to Jesse and Ruth a hundred fold, what had been bestowed on him; and the poor — how much he could help them, when he received a son's portion from the wealthy Simon! O the hearts he could make glad, all up and down the land!

The old day-dreams he used to delight in danced temptingly before him. As he stood idly beside the work-bench one afternoon, thinking of such a future, a soft step behind him made him turn. The hammer fell from his hand to the grass, as he saw the woman who came timidly to meet him.

"Why, Aunt Leah!" he cried. "What brought *you* here?"

He had not seen her since the night his Uncle Laban had driven him from home.

She drew aside her veil, and looked at him. "I heard you had been healed," she said, "and I have always wanted to come and see you, and tell you how glad I am; but my husband forbade it. Child!" she cried abruptly, "how much you look like your father! The likeness is startling!"

The discovery seemed to make her forget what she had come to say, and she stood and stared at him; then she remembered. "Rabbi Amos told me of the offer you have had from a rich merchant in Bethany, and I came down here, secretly, to beg you to accept it. In your father's name I beg you!"

Joel looked perplexed. "I hardly know what to do," he said. "Every one advises me just as you do; but I feel that they are all wrong. Surely the Master meant me as well as father Phineas and the others, when He charged us to go and preach the gospel to every creature."

A sudden interest came into the woman's face; she took a step forward. "Joel, did *you* see Him after He was risen?"

"Yes," he answered.

"Oh, I believe then that He is the Christ!" she cried. "I have thought all the time that it might be so, and the children are so sure of it."

"And Uncle Laban?" questioned Joel.

She shook her head sadly. "He grows more bitterly opposed every day."

"Aunt Leah," he asked, coming back to the first question, "don't you think He must have meant me as well as those men?"

"Oh, hardly," she said, hesitatingly, "you are so young, and there are so many others to do it; it would surely be better for you to go to Bethany."

After she had gone home, he put away his tools, and, like one in a dream, started slowly towards the mountain.

The same summer stillness reigned on its shady slopes as when the five hundred had gathered there. He climbed up near the summit, and sat down on a high stone.

To the eastward the Galilee glittered like a sapphire in the sun; Capernaum seemed like a great ant-hill in commotion. No wonder he could not think among all those conflicting voices; he was glad he had come up where it was so still.

Phineas was going away in the morning. If Joel went also, maybe he would never look down on that scene again.

Then almost as if some living voice broke the stillness, he heard the words: "Go ye into all the world, and preach the gospel to every creature!" It was the echo of the words that had fallen from the Master's lips. Nothing once uttered by that voice can ever die; it lives on and on in the ever-widening circles of the centuries, as a ripple, once started, rings shoreward through the seas.

In that instant all the things he had been considering seemed so small and worthless. He had been planning to give Simon's gold and silver to the poor; but the Master had given them His life, Himself! Could he do less?

"Inasmuch as ye have done it unto the least of these, ye have done it unto me," something seemed to say to him. Yes; he could do it for the Master's sake, for the One who had healed him, for the One who had died for him.

Then and there, high up in the mountain's solitudes, he found the path he was to follow; and then he wondered how he could have thought for an instant of making any other choice. It was the path the Master's own feet had trod, and the boy who had followed, knew well what a weary way it led.

For his great love's sake, he gave up the old ambitions, the self-centred hopes, saying, in a low tone, as if he felt the beloved Presence very near, "Oh, I want to serve Thee truly! If I am too young now to go out into all the world, let me be Thy little cup-bearer here at home, to carry the story of Thy life and love to those around me!"

The west was all alight with the glory of the sunset; somewhere beyond its burnished portals lay the City of the King. Joel turned from its dazzling depths to look downward into the valley.

He had chosen persecution and sacrifice and suffering, he knew, but the light on his face was more than the halo of the summer sunset.

As he went down the mountain to his life of lowly service, a deep peace fell warm across his heart; for the promise went with him, a staff to bear him up through all his after life's long pilgrimage: "Lo, I AM WITH YOU ALWAY, EVEN UNTO THE END OF THE WORLD!"

THE END

Selections from The Page Company's Books for Young People

THE BLUE BONNET SERIES

Each large 12mo, cloth decorative, illustrated, per volume $1.50

A TEXAS BLUE BONNET

By Caroline E. Jacobs.

"The book's heroine, Blue Bonnet, has the very finest kind of wholesome, honest, lively girlishness."—*Chicago Inter-Ocean.*

BLUE BONNET'S RANCH PARTY

By Caroline E. Jacobs and Edyth Ellerbeck Read.

"A healthy, natural atmosphere breathes from every chapter."—*Boston Transcript.*

BLUE BONNET IN BOSTON; Or, Boarding-School Days at Miss North's.

By Caroline E. Jacobs and Lela Horn Richards.

"It is bound to become popular because of its wholesomeness and its many human touches."—*Boston Globe.*

BLUE BONNET KEEPS HOUSE; Or, The New Home in the East.

By Caroline E. Jacobs and Lela Horn Richards.

"It cannot fail to prove fascinating to girls in their teens."—*New York Sun.*

BLUE BONNET—DÉBUTANTE

By Lela Horn Richards.

An interesting picture of the unfolding of life for Blue Bonnet.

A—1

THE PAGE COMPANY'S

THE YOUNG PIONEER SERIES

By HARRISON ADAMS

Each 12mo, cloth decorative, illustrated, per volume $1.25

THE PIONEER BOYS OF THE OHIO; OR, CLEARING THE WILDERNESS.

"Such books as this are an admirable means of stimulating among the young Americans of to-day interest in the story of their pioneer ancestors and the early days of the Republic." — *Boston Globe.*

THE PIONEER BOYS ON THE GREAT LAKES; OR, ON THE TRAIL OF THE IROQUOIS.

"The recital of the daring deeds of the frontier is not only interesting but instructive as well and shows the sterling type of character which these days of self-reliance and trial produced." — *American Tourist, Chicago.*

THE PIONEER BOYS OF THE MISSISSIPPI; OR, THE HOMESTEAD IN THE WILDERNESS.

"The story is told with spirit, and is full of adventure."—*New York Sun.*

THE PIONEER BOYS OF THE MISSOURI; OR, IN THE COUNTRY OF THE SIOUX.

"Vivid in style, vigorous in movement, full of dramatic situations, true to historic perspective, this story is a capital one for boys."—*Watchman Examiner, New York City.*

THE PIONEER BOYS OF THE YELLOWSTONE; OR, LOST IN THE LAND OF WONDERS.

"There is plenty of lively adventure and action and the story is well told."—*Duluth Herald, Duluth, Minn.*

THE PIONEER BOYS OF THE COLUMBIA; OR, IN THE WILDERNESS OF THE GREAT NORTHWEST.

"The story is full of spirited action and contains much valuable historical information."—*Boston Herald.*

A—2

THE HADLEY HALL SERIES
By LOUISE M. BREITENBACH

Each large 12mo, cloth decorative, illustrated, per volume $1.50

ALMA AT HADLEY HALL
"The author is to be congratulated on having written such an appealing book for girls." — *Detroit Free Press.*

ALMA'S SOPHOMORE YEAR
"It cannot fail to appeal to the lovers of good things in girls' books." — *Boston Herald.*

ALMA'S JUNIOR YEAR
"The diverse characters in the boarding-school are strongly drawn, the incidents are well developed and the action is never dull." — *The Boston Herald.*

ALMA'S SENIOR YEAR
"Incident abounds in all of Miss Breitenbach's stories and a healthy, natural atmosphere breathes from every chapter." — *Boston Transcript.*

THE GIRLS OF FRIENDLY TERRACE SERIES
By HARRIET LUMMIS SMITH

Each large 12mo, cloth decorative, illustrated; per volume $1.50

THE GIRLS OF FRIENDLY TERRACE
"A book sure to please girl readers, for the author seems to understand perfectly the girl character." — *Boston Globe.*

PEGGY RAYMOND'S VACATION
"It is a wholesome, hearty story."—*Utica Observer.*

PEGGY RAYMOND'S SCHOOL DAYS
The book is delightfully written, and contains lots of exciting incidents.

FAMOUS LEADERS SERIES

By Charles H. L. Johnston

Each large 12mo, cloth decorative, illustrated, per volume $1.50

FAMOUS CAVALRY LEADERS

"More of such books should be written, books that acquaint young readers with historical personages in a pleasant, informal way." — *New York Sun.*

"It is a book that will stir the heart of every boy and will prove interesting as well to the adults." — *Lawrence Daily World.*

FAMOUS INDIAN CHIEFS

"Mr. Johnston has done faithful work in this volume, and his relation of battles, sieges and struggles of these famous Indians with the whites for the possession of America is a worthy addition to United States History." — *New York Marine Journal.*

FAMOUS SCOUTS

"It is the kind of a book that will have a great fascination for boys and young men, and while it entertains them it will also present valuable information in regard to those who have left their impress upon the history of the country." — *The New London Day.*

FAMOUS PRIVATEERSMEN AND ADVENTURERS OF THE SEA

"The tales are more than merely interesting; they are entrancing, stirring the blood with thrilling force and bringing new zest to the never-ending interest in the dramas of the sea." — *The Pittsburgh Post.*

FAMOUS FRONTIERSMEN AND HEROES OF THE BORDER

This book is devoted to a description of the adventurous lives and stirring experiences of many pioneer heroes who were prominently identified with the opening of the Great West.

"The accounts are not only authentic, but distinctly readable, making a book of wide appeal to all who love the history of actual adventure." — *Cleveland Leader.*

SPECIAL HOLIDAY EDITIONS

Each small quarto, cloth decorative, per volume . $1.25
New plates, handsomely illustrated with eight full-page drawings in color, and many marginal sketches.

THE LITTLE COLONEL
(Trade Mark)

TWO LITTLE KNIGHTS OF KENTUCKY

THE GIANT SCISSORS

BIG BROTHER

THE JOHNSTON JEWEL SERIES

Each small 16mo, cloth decorative, with frontispiece and decorative text borders, per volume . Net $0.50

IN THE DESERT OF WAITING: THE LEGEND OF CAMELBACK MOUNTAIN.

THE THREE WEAVERS: A FAIRY TALE FOR FATHERS AND MOTHERS AS WELL AS FOR THEIR DAUGHTERS.

KEEPING TRYST: A TALE OF KING ARTHUR'S TIME.

THE LEGEND OF THE BLEEDING HEART

THE RESCUE OF PRINCESS WINSOME: A FAIRY PLAY FOR OLD AND YOUNG.

THE JESTER'S SWORD

THE LITTLE COLONEL'S GOOD TIMES BOOK

Uniform in size with the Little Colonel Series . $1.50
Bound in white kid (morocco) and gold . Net 3.00
Cover design and decorations by Peter Verberg.

"A mighty attractive volume in which the owner may record the good times she has on decorated pages, and under the directions as it were of Annie Fellows Johnston." — *Buffalo Express*.

A—10

Milton Keynes UK
Ingram Content Group UK Ltd.
UKHW040703150224
437844UK00007B/750